CIRCULAR SUPPLY CHAIN

17 COMMON QUESTIONS

How Any Supply Chain Can Take the Next Step

Deborah Dull

Cover design by Brian Gage at Pipe Tabor.

www.deborahdull.com

ISBN: 9798463191410

CONTENTS

WANT TO GRAB A DRINK?
AND EXPLORE MY MOST FAVORITE
TOPIC IN THE WHOLE WORLD?

For the past three years, I have explored Circular Supply Chains over several rounds of drinks with people from all across the globe. I have given dozens of keynotes and interviews about what the Circular Economy means for supply chain, and what supply chain means for the Circular Economy. When I travel to conferences and speak with Circular Economy experts, I am struck with one crazy realization.

Where are all the supply chain professionals?

There is a disconnect between those planning for circularity and those who will operationalize it. I see this as I split my keynoting time between:

- The circularity community: Pleading with them to include their supply chains in planning and designing for circularity.

- The supply chain community: Strongly recommending we invite ourselves to the circularity party.

The lack of supply chain professionals at the circularity party is outright bonkers, because supply chain professionals are extremely well placed to solve for circularity. As supply chain professionals, over and over again, we:

1. Identify the constraints in our supply chains

2. Optimize the system within those constraints

Circularity is a great, big, super cool chance to do what we do best. It's full of impossible constraints and complicated systems. The good news is that as supply chain professionals, we love solving "impossible" problems. Impossible problems are our favorite type. Solving for circularity is right up our alley.

But we have not been given the chance to solve for circularity, and we are not taking it upon *ourselves* to solve for it. To be fair, though, we can't solve a problem that we do not know exists. Too few supply chain professionals know about circularity, too few are aware of the consequences of continuing to operate as we do today, and even fewer realize the power we hold in the decisions we make.

When I speak about Circular Supply Chains in cities like Amsterdam, Pune, Nairobi, Sydney, Singapore, New York, and Cape Town, the questions I am asked from the supply chain professionals in the audience are similar. I love having this experience because, regardless of the languages we speak, we all speak supply chain. We connect over the woes and joys of inventory, operations, risk management, contingency plans, suppliers, contracts, rates, shortages – this is our shared language.

As supply chain professionals, we can enter any industry, learn their language, and add value. Like each product we manage, each industry has its own personality, nuances, stakeholders, terms, and acronyms. As I invite you to join me in the Circular Economy party, some of the language I use in this book will be more familiar to the circularity crowd than to you in supply chain. But fear not! You can learn these terms and use them to research, to design, to guide, to plan, to optimize – and to operationalize a model that is inevitable. One way or another, we will circulate materials through our supply chains forever. We simply don't have another option.

Will some of the ideas we explore seem pie-in-the-sky, crazy, unreachable, and impossible? Sure. We are not talking incremental change or small improvements here. Instead, we're talking full-blown, save-the-planet-to-avoid-water-wars-so-we-don't-all-die upheaval.

This book was a COVID lockdown project, so as I reference time ranges, know that "this last year" is the bewildering year that was 2020.

The style of this book is meant to be as if we are sitting down over drinks. This is not academic, nor is it peer reviewed. This is not an exhaustive guide. This is an introduction to a very cool topic that you can cruise through in a few hours. (*The time it would take us to split a bottle of wine, perhaps.*)

Now, sit back, grab a drink, and relax. As we explore circularity together, I hope you find delight in the challenge of solving for circularity and inspiration to learn more, tell a coworker, and start measuring your own operations.

Let's go circular.

INTRODUCING CIRCULAR SUPPLY CHAINS

This section lays the foundations for the rest of this book. As I introduce topics, I'll go past them fairly quickly because we'll explore them more in the following chapters.

1

WHY ARE WE TALKING ABOUT THIS?

I f you are reading this, you are probably a supply chain professional. And if you are a supply chain professional, you have probably made at least one Value Stream Map (VSM) in your life.

(If not, imagine a process flow that tracks value and waste in time, materials, and information – a decent capture of the seven wastes of Lean.)

In these VSMs, we study materials as they work their way through a value stream. These VSMs might be long (*across multiple borders and companies*) or short (*a single process inside a factory*). We've been taught to accelerate widgets through systems, to increase our inventory turns, and to achieve "first time right" quality. This drive for perfection in our processes is the north star for many supply chain professionals, and you probably think a lot about how to improve the processes that you operate or manage.

In 2020, I thought a lot about these VSMs, the one-way flow of goods, and what I've learned as a supply chain professional. And it occurred to me: Nearly everything we're taught in supply chain focuses on the *one moment* that we consider to be "perfect" and "right."

How many times have you been encouraged to contribute to the "perfect order?"

Have you seen this motivational poster in the hallways of your office before:

- Right product

- Right time

- Right location

- Right quantity

- Right quality

Here's the catch: everything we have been taught and everything we are optimizing for to get us to this "perfect" and "right" moment goes forward in a line toward the point of sale (POS). We all work together to barrel down the figurative runway toward the perfect POS moment. Depending on where you are in the value chain, the POS could be a warehouse dock, a seaport, a cash register... or anywhere in between.

This model we operate in supports what is called a *linear economy,* because the way we plan, build, ship, store, and optimize goes in a one-way direction that more or less forms a line. (*We can debate supply chain vs supply network later*.) As an industry, we have been working on perfecting this linear model for a long time. Since the Industrial Revolution in fact!

As it turns out, there are consequences of the linear economy. If we continue the way we have been operating these last 250 years, there are consequences for our supply chains, our economies, and our planet. In this section we will explore four of these consequences, so you have context as to why we are even talking about Circular Supply Chains at all.

CONSEQUENCE 1: WE ARE MISSING OUT ON VALUE

If you have been near any type of media in the last few years, you will have heard a lot about "single-use": single-use plastic, single-use packaging, single-use products.

Let's consider the consequences of single-use inside a VSM. Imagine these single-use widgets flowing along the VSM. And now imagine the processes along the value stream have achieved Six Sigma quality and nearly everything in the process makes it to that perfect POS. Then, the item is used that one, single time... then it's disposed of. The material in that item had one shot to add value, and now it's over. And we've given up on it.

Bummer.

The decision of when our value-adding items become waste is a carefully planned moment. The space between when you buy an item at the perfect POS and the time when you need another item is calculated carefully by companies. At what point will you need to come back to buy again? Is it in 15 minutes, like a paper coffee cup? A few days like an online shipping box? 10 years for a washing machine?

This concept of planning waste into our consumer lives (and supply chains, of course) is called *planned obsolescence*.

In supply chain, we're familiar with obsolescence. Our ERP systems have a special bucket for obsolescent inventory. Our economy today – the linear economy – relies on planned obsolescence to get more items through our supply chains, into the economy, and consumed. The goal in a linear economy is to get as many items consumed as possible.

In today's economy and today's supply chains and today's processes, at some point, our materials stop adding value and become waste. The consequence of this is that the materials we consider waste still have value, such as assets that could be repaired, packaging that could be reused, or spare parts that could be refurbished. Our supply chains, businesses, and national economies are missing out on value. On real money! The consulting firm Accenture estimates the Circular Economy could add $4.5 trillion in economic output by 2030. The consequence of continuing today's model is that we will continue to miss out on this additional value.

Imagine if materials could always add value.

CONSEQUENCE 2: WE ARE RUNNING OUT OF MATERIALS

100 billion tons of materials enter the global economy each year according to the thinktank Circle Economy. There are nearly 8

billion people on the planet. Compared to the 100 billion tons of materials, this means that for each person, the weight of about five cars enters the economy every year. For the most part, this material comes from the planet. The material is extracted from mines, oil drilling, or forests.

Of the 100 billion tons, 8.5 billion tons come from other supply chains. Some industries have figured out how to get materials from each other instead of from the planet. But on the whole, most of these materials come from the planet.

The consequence of using materials from the planet is that the planet is a finite space. This may sound crazy because the planet is so huge, but we are running out of materials inside the planet quicker than you may realize.

If you are familiar with basic economics, you know that the level of demand compared to the amount of supply will impact the price and availability of an item. A consequence of using materials from the planet is that we will eventually run out. As we approach the point when we do run out, prices will rise.

Let's have a look at what is happening to commodities prices. This chart is from the World Economic Forum. This is a graph of commodity prices over time starting in the 1900s through 2010. We can see a steady reduction in commodity prices thanks to technology improvements including the 2nd and 3rd industrial revolutions, application of Lean management methodologies, and global specialization.

And then, around 2000, all the hard work and progress through the 1900s is undone as commodities prices rise to a higher level than they were 100 years ago.

McKinsey Commodity Price Index[1]
Index: 100 = years 1999–2001[2]

1 Based on the arithmetic average of four commodity sub-indexes: food, non-food agricultural

items, metals, and energy.

2 Data for 2013 are calculated based on the average of the first three months of 2013.

Source: Grilli and Yang; Pfaffenzeller; World Bank; International Monetary Fund; Organisation for
Economic Cooperation and Development (OECD) statistics; Food and Agriculture Organization of
the United Nations (FAO); UN Comtrade; McKinsey Global Institute analysis

http://www3.weforum.org/docs/WEF_ENV_TowardsCircularEconomy_Report_2014.pdf

What happened?

The basics of supply and demand. (*Okay… it's far more complicated than this but bear with me for the main point here.*) Prices are going up because of both supply and demand:

- Supply: We're running out of supply within the planet.

- Demand: It continues to increase as consumers around the world are using more and the planned obsolescence around us increases.

We put these two factors together and we see an increase in commodity prices.

If you are in sourcing, this is not news to you because you experience this every day.

This next graph is a heat map of the periodic table of elements from the World Economic Forum. The darkest color indicates there is less than 50 years of that element left inside the planet. These include elements such as gold, silver, zinc, platinum, and tungsten.

Remaining years until depletion of known reserves (based on current rate of extraction)

Since the majority of inputs into our supply chains come from the planet instead of other supply chains, a consequence of today's supply chains is that commodity prices will continue to go up, and materials will become increasingly difficult to locate and procure.

Imagine we could use materials from each other instead of from the planet.

CONSEQUENCE 3: WE ARE GETTING DISRUPTED

Sometime in 2020, it is likely you came across an item that was out of stock. This happened to you both as a consumer and as a supply chain professional.

As supply chain professionals, 2020 was a tough year. Even through 2021, many of us are still trying to pull our supply chains out of deep backorders, unwind the bullwhips happening around the world, and stabilize our operations.

A consequence of today's linear operations is *even more* disruptions to our supply chains. Our supply chains are long and complex and open to risk every time materials change hands, production takes place, and plans are executed.

A consequence of the economic growth strategy of the last 30 years is long supply chains. As countries around the world specialized into specific manufacturing areas, our materials have gone on epic journeys across the globe. Each stop on their journey adds some small amount of value while cutting slivers of pennies off the cost-per-unit. The result is that materials travel a long, long way.

Edward Humes marvels at our long supply chains in his book, *Door to Door: The Magnificent, Maddening, Mysterious World of Transportation.* (*Worth a read.*) Edward researches the iPhone as one example of our long supply chains. He does the math and discovers the iPhone travels at least as far as the moon before it's ever used by a consumer - some 240,000 miles. Materials and components are gathered from Germany, Japan, USA, China, Taiwan, South Korea – and sent through shipping lanes and warehouses for processing, subassembly, assembly, and distribution.

Here's a simpler example of a pepper grinder I used. According to the package, this pepper was grown in Vietnam before it traveled 6,500 miles to South Africa, where it was packaged.

I used this pepper grinder 10,000 miles away from South Africa in Seattle, USA. We'll assume this pepper grinder was sent through at least a few warehouses or cross docks on its way from South Africa to Seattle rather than traveling on a perfectly straight journey. If that's the case, this pepper went at least 20,000 miles from farm to table. All for $2.59. Each time this pepper got on a truck or boat, crossed a border, was handled and processed – it was at risk of disruption.

We know that our supply chains are not always elegant streams of value. More often than elegant, our supply chains are a series of disconnected, independent organizations who share minimal information and optimize for only their own operations. A consequence of today's linear supply chains is that every time materials are handed off between processes, organizations, and countries, we open ourselves to disruption.

Imagine if our supply chains were shorter
and less disruptable.

CONSEQUENCE 4: WE ARE EMITTING CARBON

At this point, it's old news that the planet is warming. If it continues to warm, our food systems will fail, our forests will become deserts, and the oceans will rise.

While industrialization and technological advancements have brought incredible changes and lifted billions out of poverty, a consequence of this industrialization is the increased emission of carbon into the environment.

The kicker? By analyst firm McKinsey's math, 90% of an organization's carbon emissions come from their supply chains. And, more than half of all greenhouse gas emissions come from just eight types of supply chains. These supply chain types are: Automotive, construction, electronics, fashion, fast-moving consumer goods, food, freight, and professional services.

Look around you. Every material you see is there because a supply chain professional put it there. Every material *everywhere* came into the economy because a supply chain professional put it there. In supply chain, we are the stewards of materials and the guardian angels of inventory. If something moves, it's because we moved it. If something is produced, it's because we built it.

Supply chain professionals are in a stronger, more powerful position to impact carbon emissions than we realize. And just as our materials have product costs and carrying costs, they also have carbon costs.

Carbon accounting in modern supply chains is not equipped to measure the impact of circularity in supply chains. Today's approach to measuring carbon in supply chains is outlined in three scopes:

- Scope 1: Emissions directly from your in-sourced operations, such as emissions from factories, industrial processes, and fleets.

- Scope 2: Emissions from electricity purchased to run your operations.

- Scope 3: Emissions from everything else, split into 15 categories (*according to the Greenhouse Gas Protocol*) such as capital goods, outsourced services, product use, and so on.

As carbon accounting matures, we will see more guidance for how to measure linear versus circular operations in our Supply Chains in terms of carbon produced. Imagine carbon in a VSM next to materials, time, and information.

Imagine if our supply chains could regenerate the environment.

2

WHAT DOES SUPPLY CHAIN HAVE TO DO WITH A CIRCULAR ECONOMY?

I have a search alert set up for the term "Circular Supply Chain," so I get an email when the term is used in a news article somewhere on the internet. I look forward to these emails. I open them as soon as I see them come in. I look forward to them even though I know they will not have what I am hoping for. I hope they contain a story, or at least recognition, about Circular Supply Chains. But usually, they do not actually describe Circular Supply Chains. In these articles, the term "Circular Supply Chain" is most often used to describe the recycling economy: where a material is captured and brought back into a supply chain.

How sad.

Now, let me be clear on this. The processes needed for these materials to be captured are important. Recycling plays a role in circularity, but it is not the whole story, and it is not the first story.

It is actually the *last* story of the Circular Economy. (*It's considered the "circle of last resort" – more on that later.*)

When I get these email alerts, I want to see examples and voices and stories and... you know what it really is? I want to see a perspective saying that *the Circular Supply Chain is about more than just recycling materials!* Is it because I'm a supply chain nerd? Of course. And it's because we have a lot of work to do. That work cannot get started until we recognize what it is.

As I contemplate this, every few days when another search term alert email rolls into my inbox, it occurs to me that not many supply chain professionals are writing about Circular Supply Chains. The articles that mention Circular Supply Chains are, for the most part, not written by supply chain professionals. And given the confusion over supply chains (*even the standard, traditional, linear type*), perhaps I should not be so surprised that there is confusion over the combination of circular + supply chain. So, let's clear up the confusion.

A Circular Economy is made up of several components. Materials and supply chains are part of it. To navigate the different components, I have created a "we are here" map to show how the supply chain relates to the Circular Economy.

This is my version of these components. As circularity and its components mature, new levels of understanding, shared language, and standards will certainly develop. A new version of these components will emerge. For now, let's explore this *Venn Diagram of Circularity:*

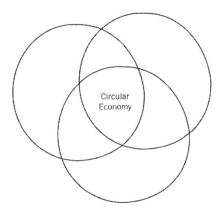

COMPONENT 1: CIRCULAR MATERIALS

As a component of the Circular Economy, materials play the starring role. The whole premise of the Circular Economy is that materials circulate because they have more value to give, and we should maximize their value for as long as possible.

We need to change the relationships we have with materials in order to get the most value from them. Today, we extract materials from the planet and keep extracting. We keep taking gold, copper, zinc, wood, petroleum, palm oil, lead, coal – you name it. Then we use those materials to make items, and we dispose of those items, declaring them no longer value-add.

But the Circular Economy says that those materials *do* add value. It's only our perspective that needs to change!

Let's start exploring the components of the Circular Economy within this key focus area of *Circular Materials*.

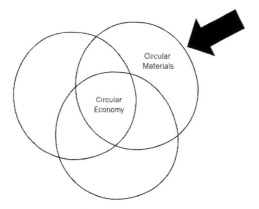

You already interact with *Circular Materials*. Consider the last time you saw any of these terms:

- Refurbished

- Repaired

- MRO (maintenance, repair, operations)

- Pre-owned

- Post-consumer

- Post-industrial

Go check out your toilet paper. The packaging should say something like "minimum 80% post-consumer recycled content" and probably next to it, "100% recycled paper." Check the tag on your t-shirt. It might say something like "100% recycled post-consumer materials." A shirt I recently bought has a label that reads "100% deadstock" which I, of course, thought was pretty cool. Have you ever bought refurbished or pre-owned electronics? All of these describe Circular Materials. When an item or material is used again, we can consider it circular.

The materials in our supply chains, as complex as they are, fall into two categories: primary and secondary. A primary material, sometimes called virgin material, comes from the planet. A secondary material has been used before and comes from another supply chain. **The idea is to reduce the amount of materials we need and then circulate the materials we use.**

When a material is used again, someone pays to use it and money enters the economy. Every time we reuse a material instead of starting from scratch (*from the planet*), we spend less time, money, energy, and emissions. This means we get a fantastic two-for-one deal: (1) materials add more money to our economies and (2) we can stop extracting these materials from the planet – and can use them from each other, instead. This means that our businesses, supply chains, and economies have a more favorable long-term forecast.

I previously shared that only 8.5% of the world's materials come from other supply chains instead of from the planet. For some, this may be depressing. But the optimistic view is this: At least it's not zero! (*Which means that someone has figured it out. A lot of someones!*) The secondary materials market is much larger than we realize.

Examples of Circular Materials:

- Reused/refurbished materials & items (first choice)

- Renewables (wind, solar power)

- Material innovations (biofacturing)

- Recycled materials (last choice)

What if every material we sourced was a Circular Material?

COMPONENT 2: CIRCULAR BUSINESS MODELS

How can we keep materials in use for as long as possible? Many argue the path is through changes in business models. A *Circular Business Model* shifts from traditional consumption-based sales models to use-based sales models. Two such business models are Product-as-a-Service (PaaS) and Sharing Platforms.

Operationally, PaaS and Sharing Platform models look almost similar. This section explores these concepts which I'll call XaaS to refer to "Anything as a Service."

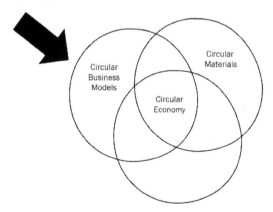

This component of the Circular Economy focuses on *Circular Business Models* that disrupt the traditional models built on planned obsolescence.

As you have gathered so far, many of today's businesses are built on planned obsolescence where the product is sold to consumers at the POS and the product is used by just one customer. The balance for companies is to minimize the product lifecycle as much as possible while still providing value to consumers.

In contrast to this model, *Circular Business Models* sell to users (*instead of consumers*), the POS is just the beginning of customer engagement (*instead of the end*), and the product is used multiple times by multiple customers (*instead of just once*). With every use of the product, money enters our businesses, supply chains, and economies.

Business models	Customer	POS is...	Product Uses
Traditional linear	Consumer	End	One time, one customer
Cooler circular	User	Beginning	Multiple times, multiple customers

The exception to the "consumer -> user" shift is food.
Circular practitioners say the only material that should be consumed is food. Everything else is used, and used, and used.

Let's explore examples of these business models. Consider a car. The average car sits parked for 92% of its life. The sales journey of this car is that it is sold to one person, and that sale generates money which enters the economy. Then, the car sits parked most of its life. Eventually, the car is sold or scrapped. In this business model, the focus is on the car.

Now consider the same car through the XaaS lens. In this business model, the focus is not on the car, but instead on the value the car brings: Transportation. Examples of XaaS are Uber, Lyft, and taxi services that sell transportation. In this model, the car is used perhaps 10 hours of the day instead of the traditional 2. Imagine the car is used by 45 riders in a day who buy Transportation-as-a-Service, and as each of those 45 riders pay for the ride, money enters the economy. In this XaaS model, the car is utilized more than in the traditional ownership model.

A premise of the Circular Economy is that a material in use is a material that is actively contributing to the economy. The more we use materials and put them to work, the more money the economy gets.

There is a business model that started over 20 years ago in the supply chain that lends itself well to *Circular Business Models*. It allows supply chains to share resources and each resource is utilized more in this model than if individual supply chains owned the resources.

Can you think of it?

Outsourced services. Consider outsourced warehousing: Multiple organizations can use the same building and pallet positions. Consider outsourced transport: 30 years ago, most supply chains owned their own fleets and managed maintenance for those fleets. Now, not only can supply chains take advantage of XaaS where the supplier manages the product (fleets), they can also participate in a Circular Economy by purchasing outsourced services.

Examples of *Circular Business Models*:

- Product-as-a-Service (supplier managed)
- Sharing economy (outsourced services)
- Reusable packaging (durable pallets)

What if our business models sold use instead of items?

COMPONENT 3: CIRCULAR OPERATIONS

How can we keep materials in use as long as possible? In the previous section, we explored changes in business models as one way to circulate materials. We can also achieve circularity through our operations.

These are, of course, not mutually exclusive approaches. We need to do both. And yet, there are thousands of circular practitioners talking about circular financing models and business models and changing consumer behavior – and not so many of us talking about *Circular Operations*.

There are two ways to tackle *Circular Operations*. First, there is an element of operationalizing circular business models (*described in the previous section*). Second, **we supply chain pros can change our operations to become circular** *even if the business model is not.*

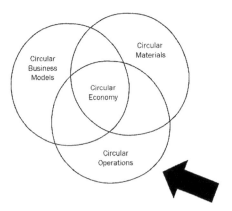

Circular Operations reduce what is needed, use materials that have been used before, and find uses for all process outputs.

Consider an XaaS model for consumers, like clothing rental. Many consider clothing rental services to be a solid example of a Circular Business Model because textiles are used again. However, many of these models are still running on top of linear operations. For example, the company may offer two-day air service for shipping the clothing and use primary materials during the cleaning process.

Now consider an XaaS model for our supply chains, like maintenance provided as part of an XaaS offering. Maintenance is critical for *Circular Operations*! However, this maintenance is linear if it is done with new spare parts created from primary materials, new lubricants and oils created from fossil fuels, more water and electricity than needed, and leverages analytics from data centers fueled with coal.

Unfortunately, many of the Circular Business Models we see today are supported with linear operations.

In most companies, the supply chain owns operations. This gives us a chance to take a critical look at how our operations are designed and optimized, and shift them to become more circular. This shift toward circularity means using fewer materials, using secondary inputs, and only creating value. This is explored further in *Chapter 3.*

Examples of *Circular Operations*:

- Operations are leaned out

- Co-locating operations such as industrial symbiosis (more on this later)

- Equipment optimization to extend use

- Water and electric use are reduced

- Oils, lubricants, and packaging are reduced then reused

What if our operations used less, used better, and used again?

~

We have covered the three main components of the Circular Economy: Circular Materials, Circular Business Models, and Circular Operations. Combining these three main components in our *Venn Diagram of Circular* will create three more components which are covered next. These next three components will be explored in terms of the challenges organizations are facing with these components.

COMPONENT 4: CIRCULAR MARKETS

Where Circular Materials and Circular Business Models meet, we find *Circular Markets*. These *Circular Markets* bring together buyers and sellers of Circular Materials.

There are market failures today that prevent supply chains and organizations from going circular. For example, the most common issue I hear from supply chains is the challenge in finding affordable and consistent sources of secondary materials.

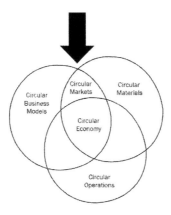

The CSCO of a CPG company told me of their woes in the secondary plastics market when a large, multi-national beverage company announced that it would begin sourcing only secondary plastics. Seemingly overnight, the existing secondary plastics became inaccessible to previous buyers in that market, like the CPG company. The market could not provide materials to all interested buyers. This represents a market failure.

As stated earlier, 100 billion tons of materials enter the global economy each year, and 8.5 billion tons come from other supply chains. One challenge in increasing that 8.5 billion number is the infrastructure in place to capture and process materials to be used again. The best way to maximize the value of materials is to reuse and repair an item (check out *Chapter 5*), but in most markets we do not have wide-scale repair, refurb, and remanufacturing facilities developed.

After items have added all the value they can, their materials are harvested and processed to be used again. The process to do this varies among countries. In the USA, much of the recycling infrastructure happens through something called Material Recovery Facilities, or MRFs (*a fun word to say, as it's pronounced "merfs"*) – and these are funded by individual counties. (*Not countries... counties... like more than a city and less than a state.*)

While advanced technology exists to separate by material type with robots and automation, the investment in this technology is often required to happen at a county level, funded by county taxes. As you can probably imagine, this is a fairly large challenge.

We do see leaders in recycling investments, such as Germany, South Korea, and Austria. Other countries, however, are struggling to create the case for investment in this infrastructure. This represents a market failure.

Our challenge is to identify these market failures and find a way around them. As supply chain professionals, we have overcome difficult operating environments and challenging constraints in our supply chains before, and this represents another chance for us to use the power of our profession to overcome market failures.

Examples of challenges in *Circular Markets*:

- Secondary materials are not available, or cost more than primary
- Infrastructure is not developed for *Circular Materials* at scale
- Policies restrict the circulation of materials

What if markets connected all supply chains to circulate materials?

COMPONENT 5: CIRCULAR STRATEGIES

Where Circular Business Models and Circular Operations meet, we find *Circular Strategies*. We use these strategies to achieve our business and operations goals.

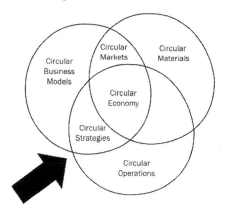

Some concepts that are commonly described as Circular Business Models, I classify as *Circular Strategies*. The difference between a business model and strategy matters to us in supply chain because it defines the degrees of freedom we have in our design and optimization.

Consider a leasing model which is considered an XaaS model. The leasing model is created, marketed, and sold to a customer. This is a Circular Business Model. Now consider a zero-waste approach, achieved through reduction and sale of process waste. This approach produces a revenue stream and is one way of achieving the business goal of profitability. This is a *Circular Strategy*.

Circular Strategies give us new options to meet our organizational targets. Examples of *Circular Strategies* include:

- Capital equipment and maintenance to meet CapEx (Capital Expense) goals.

- Co-location for more dependable material sourcing to meet cost reduction goals.

- Physically shorter supply chains to reduce emissions and meet carbon goals.

As we aim to leverage new *Circular Strategies*, we will run into challenges. We are paddling upstream against 250 years of linear economics. However, overcoming these challenges will bring benefits for our organizations (*Chapter 4*).

Examples of challenges in using *Circular Strategies*:

- Cost structures are optimized for linear flows

- Partner ecosystems often do not support *Circular Strategies*

- Traditional assumptions restrict circular scenarios from evaluation

---

What if our strategies gave us more options?

COMPONENT 6: CIRCULAR SUPPLY CHAINS

Where Circular Operations and Circular Materials meet, we find *Circular Supply Chains*.

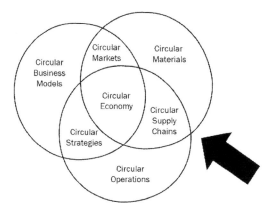

Circular Supply Chains are like ecosystems in nature. The different parts work together and are interconnected. National Geographic says that an ecosystem is "a geographic area where plants, animals, and other organisms, as well as weather and landscapes, work together to form a bubble of life." Taking this as inspiration, we can consider that Circular Supply Chains are ecosystems that work together to exchange materials to form a bubble of value. Today, we *want* our supply chains to be interconnected, and we use the term "digital supply network" and describe systems that are frictionless.

Now take an honest look at your supply chain. Is it frictionless because it's digitized and self-driving, or is it frictionless because there is a team of smart people working hard to ensure the supply chain seems like it's part of an interconnected system?

In the next chapter, I break down more details on how *Circular Supply Chains* are different from linear supply chains.

Examples of challenges in *Circular Supply Chains*:

- Operations are not connected across enterprises

- More collaboration is required for sustained operations at scale

- Systems are not optimized for material security

What if supply chains were ecosystems that only formed bubbles of value?

~

It is important to recognize the principles of the Circular Economy which I will refer to throughout this book. There are three, according to the Ellen MacArthur Foundation:

1. Design waste out of the system

2. Circulate products and materials

3. Regenerate natural systems

Another way to consider these principles is the DISRUPT model from Circle Economy's 2021 Circularity Gap Report (well worth a read). It's below (*with my commentary*):

- Design for the future (*not planned obsolescence*)

- Incorporate digital technology (*check out Chapter 14*)

- Sustain & preserve what's already there (*with smaller circulars, Chapter 5*)

- Rethink the business model (*covered in the Venn diagram above*)

- Use waste as a resource (*by turning waste streams into value streams, Chapters 9 and 10*)

- Prioritize regenerative resources (*check out Chapter 6*)

- Team up to create joint value (the *general premise of supply chain explored throughout this book*)

While all of these components impact supply chains in some way, for the rest of the book, we are here:

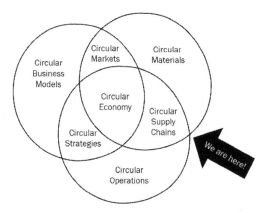

3

HOW IS THIS DIFFERENT FROM TODAY?

A s you read through the last section on the components of the Circular Economy, you may have started a mental map about how Circular Supply Chains are different from today's linear supply chains.

Let's break this comparison down together and explore the shifts from today to tomorrow.

The simplest way to describe supply chains are:

Inputs --> Process --> Outputs

As we go through this section, consider a SIPOC diagram and how each of these will shift. For simplicity, I'll collapse *supplier* with *input,* and *customer* with *output,* and we'll wrap it all in a *system.*

Let's start with the shifts from linear to circular processes.

Shift 1: From Linear to Circular Processes

We have spent years and years perfecting linear operations in our supply chains. We continuously seek portions of pennies to reduce cost, moments of activities to reduce time, and combinations of factors to improve quality. While some of the approaches to processes we use in supply chain today will carry over to supply chain tomorrow (circular), there will be shifts in our processes.

Early in my career, an executive in my supply chain talked about his approach to measuring a healthy warehouse. He would walk through the aisles of the warehouse and randomly run his finger over the top of pallets. Dust? Bad warehouse. No dust? Good warehouse. This process of measurement is based on the premise that fast movement through the supply chain is good. Inventory turns should be high.

In hanging out with Lean practitioners over the years, I have heard many versions of the "dust" story. The good news is many principles of Lean will naturally extend into circularity. But notice this shift. High inventory turns do not describe a healthy system in a Circular Supply Chain. High inventory turns means we are pushing more and more into the POS and into consumption-based linear models that are built on planned obsolescence. As we covered in *Chapter 1*, this cannot continue: we simply do not have enough material to support it.

Instead of turns, we will pursue utilization. This is because in a Circular Economy, consumers become users and, therefore, high turns become high utilization.

When we use circular processes, we can experience a wonderful part of Circular Supply Chains, which is a concept called decoupling. (*This is not the same use of decoupling as we use in supply chain to describe the push-pull point. Not confusing at all.*) Decoupling in the Circular Economy means that we can grow revenues without needing the same amount of primary material inputs. An absolute decoupling means that growth is independent from material inputs. Think about this shift like un-sticking our variable cost. As our processes shift, we will find new ways to shift our variable costs. Consider these process shifts:

- Material costs are unstuck from today's primary commodity market prices.

- Transportation and warehousing costs are eliminated and/or reduced as supply chains are shortened.

- The predominant model is one of repair and remanufacturing, which means only a small amount of new material is needed, so we spend less on materials.

- The materials we do use as inputs are secondary or renewable, which will soon be in more abundance than primary materials.

SHIFT 2: FROM LINEAR TO CIRCULAR INPUTS

Inputs are exciting because talking inputs means talking inventory, and inventory is wonderful. Some people talk about how bad inventory is for the supply chain and how it is a "necessary evil." I disagree with this. Inventory is a lovely, useful, powerful tool that allows supply chains to show up for what's needed. When used well, inventory is the make-or-break for supply chains.

The inventory that is used as inputs into linear processes are almost always primary materials. As a shift, the inventory that is used as inputs into circular processes are always secondary or renewable. Secondary materials have been used again. Renewable materials are the gifts that keep on giving, such as wind power (*wind keeps blowing*), wool (*keeps growing*). Think rapid regrowth, like using bamboo, which is a grass that can grow six inches a **day**, instead of old-growth wood that grows about six inches a **year**. We'll talk more about Circular Materials in *Chapter 5*.

The whole idea here is that we leave the items that are currently inside the planet, *inside the planet*. The extraction we have been doing has separated hundreds of billions of tons of materials from inside the planet, and nearly all of that material is sitting in landfill, in our oceans, or wandering around in the environment considered "waste." Instead of using extraction to get our inputs from inside the planet, Circular Supply Chains use what we already have.

Sound crazy? Consider the 91.5 billion tons of materials that we take from the planet every year. Now THAT is crazy!

SHIFT 3: FROM LINEAR TO CIRCULAR OUTPUTS

Think back to the VSMs of today's linear supply chains. As we make them, we find one value stream and several waste streams. Each process step produces value-added outputs and non-value-added outputs (waste).

The shift here is that in a Circular Supply Chain, each process step only produces value as outputs because waste streams become value streams! After all, we only call it *waste* today because we have not found a customer for it... yet.

Instead of value streams and waste streams, consider these to be *major value streams* and *minor value streams*.

SHIFT 4: FROM LINEAR TO CIRCULAR SYSTEMS

When we start to circulate materials among operations, we start to use a concept called industrial symbiosis. This concept started in the 1970s in Kalundborg, Denmark. It began because several factories had the same challenge of finding fresh, affordable water to use in their manufacturing processes. As a result, they created agreements to share water among the factories using pipes. For example, this connected one process that needed hot water as an input with another process that created hot water as an output. Together they formed a symbiotic system that has grown over the years and continues today. The industrial processes in Kalundborg circulate water, energy, and different materials. Collectively they save millions of euros a year and have dependable sources of material inputs from each other. The waste streams of one become the value streams of another.

Imagine this concept of industrial symbiosis and stretch it over a few hundred miles and we start to form the interconnected system that Circular Supply Chains use. These systems responsibly use technology to predict the production of both major and minor value streams, compare supply and demand needs, and exchange these materials so they can circulate and create bubbles of value.

Some supply chains are large enough to circulate materials within their own enterprise; most are not. Just as we rely on trading partners for our supply chains to be optimized today, we will rely on trading partners tomorrow.

The following definition comes from the Circular Supply Chain Network, a non-profit I started at the urging of several people I highly respect:

Circular Supply Chains are interconnected systems that use secondary and renewable inputs to create value by reducing, then maximizing, resource use.

Let's break this down, as we will be revisiting this definition several times.

Circular Supply Chains are:

- Interconnected systems, like ecosystems in nature [system]

- They use secondary and renewable inputs, not primary materials from the planet [inputs]

- They create value, not waste [outputs]

- They do this by reducing, then maximizing, resource use – like next-level Lean [process].

This table summarizes the differences in supply chain elements as we transition from linear supply chains to Circular Supply Chains:

Elements will be different	From Linear SC	To Circular SC	Circular SC Example
Inputs	Virgin, primary	Secondary and renewable	Post-industrial (reused or recycled) materials; wind power
Outputs	Value and waste	Value	Finished goods sold as "major value;" byproduct sold as "minor value"
Process	Increase inventory turnover	Reduce and maximize resources	Redesign for physically shorter operations; Lean operations; maintenance to extend capital equipment
System	Silo within and among enterprises	Interconnected like ecosystems	Data sharing on timing, quality, quantity, location of resources and material for circulation

To close out this chapter, I'll share a quote from my favorite Circular Economy OG, Walter Stahel, from his book titled *The Performance Economy.*

"The key **objective** of the circular industrial economy is to keep the economic value and utility of stocks of manufactured objects **as high as possible for as long as possible**. Use (or utilization) value is the dividend we harvest without consuming the stock themselves. **Wealth** in the circular industrial economy is measured as the sum of the quality and quantity of all stocks; **growth** is an increase in the sum of the quality of all stocks, **not an increased throughput**."

4

WHY SHOULD WE USE CIRCULAR SUPPLY CHAINS?

I get it. You have a lot going on. You have a zillion projects that are behind schedule or budget. Your supply chain is likely on fire in some way.

And yet, among all the chaos that makes up our day-to-day lives, we are asked to do more. It may be that the business we support needs financial savings, the customer wants their shipments faster, and there are processes around us that we know could be done better. We are supply chain professionals, and this is what we do. (*And let's not kid ourselves: We love it!*)

To manage our supply chains, we use the tools of our trade. We map and digitize our processes, define and redefine measures, and continuously improve our operations. From time to time, we get to imagine new ways to radically shift our operations.

Circularity gives us new tools to use while pursuing both incremental improvements and stepwise change. On the one hand, if you are looking for an ease-me-into-circularity approach, you can improve your supply chain performance by using a few of the tools that circularity introduces to our operations. On the other, if you are ready for a complete transformation, circularity is a phenomenal anchor for your work.

Circular Supply Chains see 40% cost savings when compared to linear supply chains. (*Don't believe it? Go ask Walter Stahel!*) Circular Supply Chains are resilient against risk and offer more stability and better performance over linear supply chains. Circular Supply Chains are faster, cheaper, and have higher quality than linear supply chains.

This might sound like a tall tale. Makes sense. "Circular Supply Chain" is a new concept for all of us. And as we look closely at the principles of circularity, we will find that it supercharges many of the concepts we have been using for years in supply chain.

Let's explore five benefits of Circular Supply Chains.

BENEFIT 1: CIRCULAR SUPPLY CHAINS ARE SHORTER

I know what you're thinking: "Short is not a benefit." Stick with me here.

Today, our supply chains are long and disruptable. We send our inventory on epic journeys: To travel thousands of miles in search of low-cost labor for the next "value-added" activity in a long series of "value-added" journey stops. Imagine if we could remove the transportation, boxing and unboxing, loading and unloading, quality inspections between processes, and border crossings. If we can do this (*Hint: We definitely can!*), then we remove the source of many types of risk through the supply chain: Travel.

Circular Supply Chains operate regionally, which means they locate, harvest, transform and use materials all within a relatively small geographical area (*let's call it 350 miles*). Keeping our materials close to our operations is a strategic benefit as we consider the upcoming material scarcity that is on our collective horizon. Shorter supply chains give us the benefit of more dependable supply.

Shorter supply chains also allow us to save time and money because we don't have to start from scratch every time.

We can save time because we don't start from a mine, oil rig, or forest and go through every step of the long value chain. Instead, imagine we start with an item that has already been made and we refurbish, remanufacture, or repurpose it. Shorter supply chains give us the benefit of faster, more responsible supply chains.

In addition to time savings, we can save money if we don't have to go through all the steps of extraction and processing and shipping around the world. The benefit of this is that even with our operational cost savings, the customer is still willing to pay a relatively high amount. There is a decoupling between what it costs us, and what we can charge to our customers. Shorter supply chains give us the benefit of lower costs and higher margins.

(If you're thinking "Yes, but…," please go back to Chapter 2 and the component on Circular Markets where I acknowledge that yes, there are market failures which means access to secondary materials and proper infrastructure are not developed to where they need to be. Yet.)

Shorter supply chains also help address a consequence of linear supply chains that we explored in Chapter 1: Emissions. Shorter supply chains ship fewer goods around the world, and therefore emit less carbon. If your supply chain is like many supply chains these days, you have recently committed to a carbon-reduction target in your operations. Many supply chain executives I speak with are looking for ideas on how to reduce their carbon footprint. Shorter supply chains are a fantastic starting point, because shorter supply chains give us the benefit of fewer carbon emissions.

These shorter supply chains give us benefits in our operation because they have more dependable supply, are faster, are cheaper, and emit less carbon.

BENEFIT 2: CIRCULAR SUPPLY CHAINS ARE LEANER

The first principle of the Circular Economy is to use less and design waste out of our processes. This principle may remind us of the ongoing work we do with Lean to continuously explore and improve our operations by reducing wasted time, effort, motion, and materials. Many of our processes have already completed extensive process analysis to reduce quality issues, scrap, and rework.

You are likely familiar with the benefits of running a Lean operation. Using less means saving time and money. Cleaner workspaces and diligence in work instructions means higher quality. Applying Lean to the digitization of our processes means cleaner master data and the ability to use the data we produce to improve our processes even more.

The circular mindset is a natural extension of the Lean mindset. If Lean is about finding and *eliminating* waste, then circularity is about finding and *monetizing* it. Circularity also extends the benefits of Lean.

If Lean is about finding and eliminating waste, then circularity is about finding and monetizing it.

Monetizing industrial waste is nearly a $60-billion-a-year industry in the United States. Our supply chains are already harvesting materials throughout our value chains because it makes financial sense. These harvesting operations will experience incredible growth in the coming years. As more supply chains circulate more materials back into other supply chains and commodities markets, the availability of secondary materials will increase and we can reduce our strain on the planet while increasing dependability of supply. Exciting!

These leaner supply chains give us benefits in our operations because reducing waste saves time and money, and monetizing waste introduces new revenue streams.

BENEFIT 3: CIRCULAR SUPPLY CHAINS ARE BETTER CONNECTED

If I say "digital transformation" does it make you want to close this book? I get it. But please don't.

Our supply chains have been on a digitization journey these last few years. We have debates on digital vs. digitized and supply chains vs. digital networks. We have spent a lot of money on various digital initiatives. Some have worked and some have not. It's all been quite an undertaking.

Successful digital initiatives connect the digital capabilities with a business outcome. Circular Supply Chains require a certain level of digitization to connect supply chains and material movement. This can provide a rationale for further digital investments and can provide purpose to the digital initiatives that have happened so far.

Consider the minor value (*waste*) that every operation in the world produces. This minor value becomes a source of raw materials for another operation in the world (*as a secondary material input*). In order for this exchange to happen, we need to know a lot about those materials such as characteristics, quantity, location, availability, and quality. To have this level of detail across all materials in our operations, we need to rely on digital solutions. (*Remember: 100 billion tons of material enters the global economy each year.*)

Circular Supply Chains are connected so that materials can be analyzed and exchanged. These connected supply chains form the basis of the ecosystems that create bubbles of value. In addition to sharing information with our trading partners to assist in forecasting and planning like we do today, our supply chains will also need to know about the materials we circulate with each other through our value chains.

It can be a challenge to get data from our partners today. However, there is more willingness to share data when the reason for the data exchange and use of the data becomes more explicit. Leveraging circular initiatives as a catalyst for data exchanges gives an opening and first step to creating digital foundations for Circular Supply Chain ecosystems.

These better-connected supply chains give us benefits in our operation because they allow for materials exchanges across our interconnected supply chains.

BENEFIT 4: CIRCULAR SUPPLY CHAINS ARE MORE FLEXIBLE

Your supply chain scorecard might measure flexibility, or it might measure adaptability or agility. Regardless of what we call it, this scorecard item measures how well we can manage the impacts of the changes around us. Circular Supply Chains will have a new source of change and reason to be flexible: input materials.

Today, we define the inputs that our processes need in terms of specs in the Bill of Materials (BOM). Tomorrow, we will define the inputs in a new way. In our BOMs, we will use characteristics such as viscosity, ability to conduct heat, and malleability; and we will define tolerance ranges for these characteristics. As materials remain regional, the benefit of this flexibility is that we will have more options for inputs than if we stick to today's strict specs.

The *Excess Materials Exchange* in Amsterdam is developing a concept they call the *Periodic Table of Uses,* which aims to show materials in terms of these characteristics rather than in their pure chemical make-up like the periodic table of elements does today. This reference will allow material scientists, designers, engineers, and supply chain professionals to expand potential input materials which gives our supply chains more flexibility.

These flexible supply chains give us benefits in our operation because they allow us to take in a wider range of process inputs which gives us more options to mitigate the changes around us.

BENEFIT 5: CIRCULAR SUPPLY CHAINS ARE MORE PREDICTIVE

Predicting what happens in our supply chains today is complicated. Circularity will bring new value streams, new customers, and new suppliers that we need to predict and manage. At first, it may seem that a Circular Supply Chain will be more difficult to predict. Instead, circularity brings the benefit of better prediction to our operations.

As we have already covered, Circular Supply Chains are shorter. They travel shorter distances and have fewer opportunities to be disrupted. This also brings a benefit to our ability to predict. If there are fewer containers, pallets, and boxes traveling, and they are traveling fewer miles, our prediction math can take fewer factors into consideration.

Next, we explored changes to process inputs. Inputs will vary more widely than they do today as our materials and source of materials begin to change. While this introduces new variables it also provides more planning options and contingency plans so our operations can continue. Predicting these supply chain inputs allows us to focus on prioritizing viable options rather than only predicting disruptions. This is a benefit as we predict multiple paths rather than one path with multiple risks.

Finally, Circular Supply Chains have major value streams and minor value streams. Today, we predict the major value streams and provide the results of our predictions to our customers and to our suppliers so the value chain can operate. Tomorrow, our minor value streams will create new customers and those customers will need predictions to manage their supply plans. If we have already laid the groundwork to measure our outputs, a benefit of a Circular Operation is that the prediction needed by these minor value stream customers will have already been created.

These predictive supply chains give us benefits in our operation because shorter supply chains are easier to predict, predicting circular inputs focuses on prioritizing across many operations rather than protecting our few options, and minor value stream predictions nearly create themselves.

--

This section introduced Circular Supply Chains to offer context and validity to the rest of this book. In the next section, we'll begin our exploration with the inputs of Circular Supply Chains.

Inputs of Circular Supply Chains

Circular Supply Chains are interconnected systems that *use secondary and renewable inputs* to generate value by reducing, then maximizing, resource use. This section explores the secondary and renewable inputs we use in Circular Supply Chains.

5

WHAT IS A CIRCULAR MATERIAL?

The name "Circular Economy" comes from materials circulating through our supply chains. Circular Materials can describe materials and resources that:

• Have been used before (**secondary**), like harvested spare parts

• Are available ongoing (**renewable**), like wind

• Are grown with minimal negative impacts (**biomaterials**), like algae

• Improve the environment (**regenerative**), like carbon capture

Two notable items: (1) It is common to see the phrase "Secondary Materials" used as an umbrella term for all types of Circular Materials. (2) "Rapidly Renewable" means

*something can grow back within ten years and is generally
accepted as a Circular Material, depending on the growing
process used.*

Some materials, like water or glass, could fall into different categories depending on the situation. Water may seem to be renewable until we find ourselves in a drought. At that point, water should be considered a secondary material that is treated and used again and again. The glass for our cell phone or computer screens may seem like a secondary material that is used again until it can be grown with new material science. At that point, it becomes a biomaterial.

Regardless of their type or situation, Circular Materials move in circles. These circles can be small or big.

- A smaller circle means less is done to that material. For example, a reusable shipping pallet that is used by many supply chains.

- A larger circle has more processing. For example, the shipping pallet needs to be repaired and then is used again.

The idea is to keep the smallest circle possible; to leave an item as itself for as long as possible. In supply chain, we think about materials in terms of lifecycle stages. Let's explore five lifecycle stages, starting with the smallest circle, and use an industrial robot as an example.

LIFECYCLE STAGE 1: REUSE

Our lifecycle stage story starts with the idea of *Reuse*. In a Circular Supply Chain, imagine that everything has been used before, so it will be uncommon to just have "use."

The industrial robot in our supply chain is reused over and over. It may be sold to another supply chain and reused in their process. During *Reuse*, it is reviewed with sensors and math. This gives the supply chain the information needed to complete prescriptive maintenance. If this robot is used as part of an XaaS offering, then the leasing company will monitor its performance from a distance and provide remote or on-site maintenance as needed.

Because *Reuse* is the smallest circle in a Circular Supply Chain, it is important that the robot stays in this lifecycle stage for as long as possible. The robot adds the most value in this lifecycle stage and it takes effort, time, and money to bring it from a larger circle back to this lifecycle stage.

LIFECYCLE STAGE 2: REPAIR AND REFURB

The next lifecycle stage happens when the robot cannot continue to add value and needs to be repaired or refurbished.

In this lifecycle stage, for the robot to be repaired it will need planning, inputs, and expertise for the repair to happen. The best time for repair to happen is for it to be scheduled during planned downtime so that the rest of the process isn't interrupted. This is because all of the other equipment in the process should be utilized as much as possible.

LIFECYCLE STAGE 3: REMANUFACTURE

Remanufacture is needed when an entire module needs to be replaced for the robot to continue to be used.

The replacement module is a refurbished module taken from another robot during remanufacturing and repaired so it can be reused. The ideal way to do this is to replace the module while leaving the rest of the robot in place, so that the process has minimal impact from downtime. Then the module can be taken to a repair facility and prepared for reuse by another robot.

The replacement module is a refurbished module, taken from another robot during remanufacturing and repaired so it can be reused.

This is a larger circle because more effort, time, money, and materials will go into the robot in order to return it to the Reuse lifecycle stage.

LIFECYCLE STAGE 4: REPURPOSE

The *Repurpose* lifecycle stage happens when a component or module can no longer add value in its current state. It may be that the component has been damaged in some way.

The goal of this lifecycle stage is to harvest viable components and repair them for reuse. Whereas the Remanufacture lifecycle phase leaves a module intact and repairs it, Repurpose breaks an item down to its component parts. These parts are refurbished and put into a spare parts inventory.

Industry standards means that some of these spare parts may be used by different equipment in different processes. While some of the refurbished spare parts may return to the original robot, this is not required.

LIFECYCLE STAGE 5: RECYCLE

The last lifecycle stage, and the largest circle, is *Recycle*. It is the largest circle because it requires the most effort and inputs. Some materials don't recycle well and lose quality each time they are recycled.

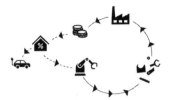

During *Recycle*, components are processed down to their material level. These materials are then gathered and sold into the commodities markets, which feed multiple industries. It may be that some portion of the robot makes it back to the same process, but this is not a requirement.

It's worth noting that there are innovations in recycling technologies that will help us transition from linear to circular materials. Advanced recycling focuses on giving today's materials another shot at adding value.

A NOTE ON INPUTS

The above pictures are simple lifecycle diagrams. As supply chain professionals, we know that in each step different types of Circular Materials are used as inputs.

For example, as our robot is maintained, it may need lubricants, water, and analytics that are done in the cloud. For this to be a Circular Operation, these inputs need to be Circular Materials. Imagine:

- Lubricant is a synthetic lubricant that was created using carbon capture (regenerative)

- Water is from the process watershed that is processed and reused on-site (secondary)

- An analytics cloud provider runs a Circular Data Center (secondary, renewable)

We are aware of the complexity of process inputs across our value chains. We are aware because we plan, move, manage, analyze, and optimize these inputs and processes. Our value stream maps will expand to include tracking material types so we can measure what is primary material and what is a secondary material.

~

In researching this, you will come across various depictions of Circular Materials including the butterfly diagram. They all have the same spirit and essence. Approach these with a supply chain lens, so you can analyze your processes.

6

WHERE CAN I GET CIRCULAR MATERIALS?

This is one of the top two most frequent questions I am asked about Circular Supply Chains:

Where in the world can I even get Circular Materials?

Given the novelty of the concepts around Circular Supply Chains and the different language used to describe Circular Materials, this presents us with a challenge. Challenging...but not impossible. Not for us in supply chain, anyways.

Circular Materials are already in our supply chains today, and they make up less than 10% of the 100 billion tons of materials that enter our global economy each year, so we have work ahead of us if we want to get to 100%.

And who buys those 100 billion tons of material each year?

Supply chain professionals.

Yup, this one's on us.

Now let's identify six possible sources of Circular Materials.

SOURCE 1: CIRCULAR MATERIALS FROM YOUR OWN SUPPLY CHAIN

One source of Circular Materials is from within our own four walls. Our supply chains produce outputs and byproducts, and these can be used again.

The chemical company BASF has leaned into this concept in six Verbund sites around the world. These sites are all using the idea of industrial symbiosis to exchange materials among manufacturing processes. These Verbund sites are seen as "*the intelligent interlinking of production plants, energy flows and infrastructure*" and have helped BASF's supply chain to be recognized among the world's most innovative. While increasing their material security, they also save over a billion euros. Every year.

BASF has the advantage of managing a large supply chain, but the principles of what they use for their Verbund sites can be used by any size of supply chain. One of these principles is to look for materials to use again in your own supply chain.

We have, of course, done this for years. We use up inventory before buying new. (*We try to, anyway.*) We take care of our equipment with MRO and refurbished spare parts. We reuse pallets and packaging when it's possible. We sometimes even treat water on site and use it again through our processes. Running a

Circular Supply Chain means expanding what we're already doing and applying it throughout our processes.

Does your supply chain produce waste streams that could be candidates to become minor value streams?

SOURCE 2: CIRCULAR MATERIALS DIRECT FROM OTHER SUPPLY CHAINS

In a Circular Economy, every supply chain is the source of raw materials for another supply chain. We could imagine this to be like taking the BASF Verbund sites and expanding it across different companies. An example of this is in the Kalundborg Symbiosis, which is made of a series of bilateral agreements among different supply chains.

The CPG company Procter & Gamble has pursued a zero-waste-to-landfill strategy for over ten years, saving more than $2 billion. They have avoided sending 5 million tons of waste to landfills and have also created revenue streams for the company by selling out-of-spec products to other supply chains. For example, they sell out-of-spec soap to car washes. This has multiple benefits:

- Avoiding a scenario where material never adds value to the economy and goes to landfill
- Saving money spent on disposal
- Reducing the carbon footprint
- Creating a revenue stream for the company

If you operate a zero-waste-to-landfill operation, you are familiar with the approaches needed to find a value-adding home for your minor value streams. Imagine that 100% of our outputs will be used again.

How much money could you save if you didn't have to pay to dispose of anything in your supply chain?

Source 3: Circular Materials from Commodities Markets

It is possible to get Circular Materials from the market. Commodities markets already include post-industrial and post-consumer materials. Brokers and marketplaces have emerged in different markets to connect supply chains.

One example is the asset management and marketplace company Rheaply which offers supply chains the chance to extend the life of their assets, and then sell them to others. By anchoring in circularity, Rheaply uses the principles of connected systems and material stewardship. By leaving items as themselves rather than harvesting them for parts or materials, the item adds more value to our supply chains. Smaller circles add more value!

As supply chain professionals like you go into the market and inquire about Circular Materials, more Circular Materials will emerge. We are the buyers, and our demand signals will shape the market.

Go forth and demand signal!

How much of your commodities purchases are primary vs.
secondary materials?

SOURCE 4: CIRCULAR MATERIALS OUT OF THE ENVIRONMENT

Last time you went to buy laundry detergent, did you see a bottle with an announcement on the front that read *"MADE WITH OCEANS PLASTICS"*? These last few years, companies are taking plastic from the ocean and turning it into pellets for bottles, yarns for fabrics, and beads for bracelets.

The technology company Hewlett-Packard creates ink and toner cartridges from Circular Materials including ocean plastics. They have captured over 200 million pounds of plastic from the environment to put into their supply chain.

If we can interrupt the flow of materials before it ends up out in the environment, then we can participate in a concept called urban mining. The idea is to reuse materials from cities and put them back into a supply chain. Four billion people live in cities today, which is just over half the people on the planet. These people are using materials every day. Imagine if our short supply chains that operate regionally could source Circular Materials from the cities that they serve?

In 2020, I was interviewed by *Procurement with Purpose* and claimed we would be mining landfills by 2050. Mark my words: Full-on WALL-E style robots processing our landfills will happen in our lifetime. We send billions of tons of materials to landfills each year and most of that continues to sit underground, in the same condition it was in when we put it there. The technology is advancing to give us the capability to process mixed waste into commodities with high enough quality to pass for primary materials. Today, landfills add no value to our supply chains. Landfills are making the planet *worse* by emitting carbon. In the next twenty years (maybe even ten!), we'll see landfills mined. The materials in them are just too valuable to leave there.

If you could access any material from the environment, what would it be?

SOURCE 5: CIRCULAR MATERIALS FROM NATURE

This can be a touchy subject. Since the third principle of the Circular Economy is to regenerate natural systems, then how can nature be a source of Circular Materials?

Let's consider the materials that come to mind first: solar power and wind power. Now consider natural materials that regenerate rapidly (within 10 years) like bamboo, cork, flax, hemp, kelp, and wool. These materials can be tricky because, depending on how they are grown and their value chains – they can actually do more harm than good for the planet. In other words, their carbon emissions are higher than any benefit they provide.

The word *"sustainable"* was first used in 1713 by – get this – the mining industry. A fellow called Hans Carl Von Carlowitz sat down and did the math on how much timber could be used to support his mining process. His goal was to take so few trees that the forest would continue to produce trees, so he could continue to have trees to use. The key here is to use so little of the natural resource that it will continue to produce and regenerate.

We seem to have forgotten this important concept as we have industrialized because we clean-cut forests and extract everything a mine has inside. The problem for us in supply chain is that clearing out natural resources adds a high level of risk into our supply chains because it means we must continuously seek new sources of raw materials.

Have a critical look at your materials to identify the impact they have as they are taken from the planet.

In your supply chain, what material do you use most of? How quickly can it regenerate?

SOURCE 6: CIRCULAR MATERIALS FROM BIOLOGY

Circular Materials made with biology are a new approach, using biomanufacturing (or shortened to biofacturing). This is a new space. We see examples emerging from a few interesting companies that are worth keeping an eye on.

One pioneer in this space is Ecovative. They have taken on plastic foam packaging. Instead of a petroleum-based product that never breaks down, they have created a packaging that can be grown in under a week and breaks down with composting in about a month. How do they do it? With agriculture byproducts and mushroom spores. First, they press the agriculture byproduct (like corn husks) into the packaging shape. Then they insert mushroom spores and biology takes over. About a week later, they have packaging that is competitive with traditional foam packaging on both cost and functionality.

An important focus for the growing technology breakthroughs in biomanufacturing will be to make sure they use Circular Operations as they pursue these exciting Circular Materials, so that all inputs into the process are circular.

Have you explored using biomanufacturing to source materials?

\-\-

This section has explored inputs we use in Circular Supply Chains. In the next section, we'll continue our exploration with the processes of Circular Supply Chains.

PROCESSES OF CIRCULAR SUPPLY CHAINS

As we kick off this section, a reminder that Circular Supply Chains are interconnected systems that use secondary and renewable inputs to generate value by *reducing, then maximizing, resource use*. This section explores the processes we use in Circular Supply Chains that reduce, then maximize, resource use. We'll explore smaller circles, Lean, and shorter supply chains.

7

WHAT DO SMALLER CIRCLES MEAN FOR MY SUPPLY CHAIN?

In a Circular Supply Chain, a smaller circle means less effort, materials, cost, time is put into a good before it can be used again. As we covered in *Chapter 5,* the smallest circle is reuse and the largest circle is recycling.

As the world shifts toward a Circular Economy and our supply chains start to compete on smaller circles, this will impact how we operate. Let's explore four effects of smaller circles on our supply chains.

EFFECT 1: POINT OF SALE IS JUST THE BEGINNING

We get excited about the point of sale (POS). A customer sale means the supply chain has succeeded in planning, building, moving, and supplying an item that is needed by the customer. Happy day!

Today, this POS moment is the end of the road. We have been successful in delivering the product. On the other hand, in the land of smaller circles, this POS moment is just the beginning of the relationship we have with the customer. We will repair this item for the customer and make sure it lasts a long time. When this customer is done with the item, we will refurbish it and sell it to another customer.

Shifting to XaaS models is interesting from a business perspective because we have a continuous source of revenue. XaaS leads to smaller circles because items are used over and over again.

Consider the effect on supply chains of selling heavy equipment, compared to leasing it, compared to offering it as a service.

If you are already managing an XaaS supply chain today, you have a head start. If not, now is a great time to start reading up about the differences in managing an XaaS supply chain rather than a traditional product sale supply chain.

EFFECT 2: REPAIR MORE THAN BUILDING NEW

In a Circular Supply Chain, we will inevitably repair more than we repair today. Single use just cannot continue!

Consider Loop from TerraCycle. Their goal is to replace single-use containers. At first it seemed like an impossible journey to tackle single-use packaging at fast food restaurants. In 2020, Loop announced partnerships with Burger King and Tim Horton's to trial reusable packaging.

In supply chain, this means we need to be ready to support these new operations. It is not a small shift to transition from providing single-use products to servicing reusable products through cleaning, repair and reuse.

What does this mean for us? An initial brainstorm says:

- Materials coming into our supply chains will shift from linear to circular. These materials will either come from new suppliers, or our current suppliers will make a transition to source different items for us.

- The use of asset management will expand. No longer reserved for capital equipment, we'll have a better idea of where individual items are as they circulate through the economy and back into our supply chains.

- Inventory management will be awesome. (*Let's be honest, it's already pretty great.*) I predict that some level of convergence will happen between asset management and inventory management as we apply lessons from reusable beverage containers, shipping containers, and pallets to new parts of our supply chains.

Take a moment to imagine the effect if every item in your operation was repaired rather than purchased new.

EFFECT 3: SLOWER INVENTORY TURNS

Inventory is so interesting. Today, we use inventory turns as a sign of health in the supply chain. Higher turns mean more movement and more movement means a healthier operation.

Inventory turns are normally calculated financially. We say that once we turn materials into money from the customer, we get a turn. This is calculated by comparing some sort of sales number (either sales or COGS, depending on which philosophy your supply chain uses) against the value of the inventory on hand.

With this math, higher is better because it means our sales of products are high. What happens, though, when we move from consumption to use?

Depending on how we do the math, our inventory turns will either be dismal or pretty great. Let's break this down.

First, to calculate inventory turns, we need average inventory value and COGS. *(Where COGS is made up of direct costs: material, labor, factory overhead, and so forth.)*

Start with COGS. In a linear supply chain with traditional product sales; this is straightforward math. However, in a Circular Supply Chain with small circles, our COGS will be lower. This is because we will do less to the item to prepare it for resale. Where a linear supply chain starts at the planet, a Circular Supply Chain (*focusing on the smallest circle*) starts with an item that already exists.

Now, a look at inventory. In a linear supply chain, the inventory value used for COGS and inventory is usually the same. In a Circular Supply Chain, however, it is not. The direct cost that goes into an item to prepare it for resale is not the same as the inventory value.

In plain language, what this all means is the way we measure health in our supply chains is about to get a little shaken. Utilization becomes the metric to use in a Circular Supply Chain instead of inventory turns. But today, we place a lot of value on inventory turns and days on hand.

Take a moment to consider the effect if we changed this key performance metric.

EFFECT 4: SHORTER WAIT TIMES

Smaller circles mean we operate regionally and rapidly. If utilization is a critical metric instead of inventory turns, we want to make sure that the items are used all the time. As we increase use, we will increase MRO. All of you working in MRO today will become superheroes to the rest of the supply chain, because your world is about to become the center of our operations.

If our operations do not need to start from the planet each time, we can move more quickly. Imagine we can leverage existing spare parts, finished goods, and recycled materials. Instead of a months-long process starting with a mine or refinery, we can move in weeks, days, or hours. This applies if we are reusing, repairing, or remanufacturing – or even building new.

What if we didn't have to start from scratch each time?

8

I'VE ALREADY LEANED OUT MY SUPPLY CHAIN. HOW IS THIS DIFFERENT?

I earned my Six Sigma Green Belt in the first year of working at Microsoft. I was enamored by the structured process to improve any process and since then, I have collected wise guidance from Six Sigma, Lean, and Kaizen practitioners.

There is some debate on the difference between Lean and Kaizen. To me, Lean focuses on reducing waste (*usually those 7 deadly types*) and Kaizen looks at improving 3 Mus: Muda, Mura, and Muri.

Circular thinking is an expansion and extension of Lean or Kaizen thinking. This section explores the similarities and differences between Circular Supply Chain and Kaizen.

SIMILARITY & DIFFERENCE 1: MUDA (7 WASTES)

Think back to the value stream map. As we create these maps and analyze the As-Is or Current State view, we look at the map with a lens to scan for the 7 wastes (many include an 8th waste of wasted talent, but I will stick to the traditional 7): Inventory, waiting, motion, transport, defects, overproduction, and over-processing. These wastes are activities that are not value-added, meaning that the customer will not pay for them.

There are similarities between Circular Supply Chain and Muda because of the first principle of the Circular Economy, which is to *design waste out of the system.* There are a few differences, as well.

Inventory hides an inefficiency or problem somewhere in the process or the supply chain. There is too much inventory in our supply chains today, because they are long and have more nodes that are required. Add a node, add inventory. A similarity between Kaizen and circularity is that both aim to reduce inventory. The Circular Economy will require less inventory because single-use consumption moves to multi-use utilization. Our items will be repaired and used over and over.

Waiting is time that should be filled with value-added activity but is stalled because of resource availability. A similarity between Kaizen and circularity is to reduce waiting, because the second principle of the Circular Economy is to keep materials in use. *Waiting* in a process means that a process that is filled with items (equipment) is not adding value to the economy. *At the same time,* there is a difference. It is important to note that in a linear supply chain *Waiting* is Muda because we want higher turns. However, a Circular Supply Chain is not optimizing for turns. It is optimizing instead for utilization. It may seem like splitting hairs, but this difference is an important concept to grasp so we can put proper measurements in place.

Motion occupies our inventory in between value-added steps and means that other items (equipment) in the process are idle and not adding value, and *Transport* is bigger motion (ha). Another similarity here, because Circular Supply Chains are short and regional and eliminate much of the transport seen in today's linear supply chains.

Defects create unnecessary scrap due to poor quality. This means that the material is likely never used by anyone and is scrapped instead. It never had a chance to add value! A similarity between Kaizen and circularity is a focus on quality. In a Circular Supply Chain, quality is improved, items are repaired, and scrap is repurposed back into the supply chain.

Over-processing puts more effort into the inventory than the customer requires. This is an interesting difference between Kaizen and circularity. While we do not want to spend money that is not necessary, there may be circumstances in a Circular Supply Chain where we will put in more functionality into a product than an individual user requires. For example, imagine an XaaS offering where a user could enjoy the offering for an hour, or for a week or more. Functionality requirements will vary across users. To enable the XaaS business model, it may seem that we are *over-processing*.

Overproduction is at the heart of the linear economy. In supply chain today, we make more inventory than what is needed. This excess is created so that it can be discounted later and sold on to a consumer. In a Circular Supply Chain, we end our reliance on planned obsolescence. A similarity between Kaizen and circularity is that it focuses on eliminating *overproduction*.

SIMILARITY & DIFFERENCE 2: MURA (UNEVENNESS)

In supply chain, we are not fans of variation. Variation is not awesome! It's hard to predict and plan for, which means we end up spending more money and time than necessary. It means we need to run more scenarios to try to account for variation and unevenness.

Linear supply chains focus on reducing variation. They like to produce an even number of items across an even number of shifts in a month. Linear supply chains build new items, evenly and continuously.

On the other hand, Circular Supply Chains repair a lot of items rather than building new ones. Repair, refurbish, and remanufacture may introduce unevenness into the operation because we cannot always correct for the variation that comes from changes in user behavior. This is an interesting difference between Kaizen and circularity.

Circular Supply Chains also use variable inputs (as we explored in *Chapter 4*), which will result in some level of Mura due to changes needed to accommodate for different types of inputs.

While the spirit of Mura is a similarity between Kaizen and circularity, Circular Supply Chains ensure that equipment is used in an even manner so they can have long lifecycle phases. On the other hand, a difference between Circular Supply Chains and Kaizen is that Circular Supply Chains will introduce some Mura into our processes.

SIMILARITY & DIFFERENCE 3: MURI (OVERBURDEN)

Muda, Mura, and Muri and Japanese words. The Japanese kanji for Muri translates into "totally unreasonable." Muri is expecting totally unreasonable performance from the people and machines in our supply chains.

This is a great topic to explore. The second principle of the Circular Economy says to "*keep materials in use.*" When we apply this principle to the equipment in our operations, we know it's a balance to increase the use of the equipment while also stopping use of equipment for maintenance from time to time. Muri is a similarity between Kaizen and circularity.

Our buddy Walter Stahel explores this, too. He finds that "*the circular industrial economy substitutes manpower for energy and resources ... [and] the linear industrial economy substitutes energy (machines) for manpower.*" Wow. So... our current, linear operating approach is all about removing the need for manpower because we have the power of steam and machines. (*The power of steam and machines was the major addition to society of the first industrial revolution*). And now the Circular Supply Chain says to bring back manpower? And that we won't lose all our jobs to robots?

Bingo.

If we need to repair more often than we build new, we need a lot of skilled labor in our supply chains. (*Spoiler alert: Lot size 1 is coming, and it may not be what you think.*)

Similarity & Difference 4: We Need Another Mu

I propose a new Mu.

Consider any process and imagine the major and minor value streams that it produces. The minor value stream could be a new type of Mu.

Here are a few examples:

- Beer brewing results in "spent grains" that have given up their sugar but are still nutritious. The folks at ReGrained take this byproduct and create snack bars out of it.

- Desalination processes exist to create drinking water from salt water. They create salt as a byproduct which can also be used.

- Carbon dioxide produced as a byproduct can be used to carbonate beverages.

How do we describe these symbiotic relationships that are forming, regionally, among supply chains around the world? We need a word that means "waste that isn't waste." I propose a new Mu!

Take a few moments and imagine one of your most critical processes. What could happen if we explore these Mu wastes with a Circular lens?

9

CAN WE MAKE OUR SUPPLY CHAINS SHORTER?

There are assumptions we make as supply chain professionals about our supply chains. Sometimes they are so consistently present, that we consider them to be "truths." And sometimes, we confuse assumptions with constraints.

A good supply chain professional differentiates truths from constraints from assumptions. We push on our constraints periodically, so we can confirm which are constraints and which are actually assumptions. This makes a difference for us because it means we have different degrees of freedom to optimize performance depending on working with assumptions versus constraints.

When I worked at the Bill & Melinda Gates Foundation, I spent my first year listening to professionals working in health supply chains in Africa, Europe, and America. I listened for clues about constraints versus assumptions. All supply chains have their own assumptions and constraints, and the supply chains that move pharmaceuticals into frontier markets have theirs as well. How often do you challenge yours?

The spoiler to the question of *"Can we make our supply chains shorter?"* is that yes, of course we can. But to do it, we must face and challenge four of our long-held assumptions. As we go through these four, consider if you hold any of these assumptions for your own supply chain.

ASSUMPTION 1: CENTRALIZED IS OPTIMIZED

We have spent decades centralizing, specializing, and optimizing for cost. Global supply chains have chased low-cost labor around the world in an effort to compete on cost and sell more to consumers to fuel our linear economy. It is this pursuit of low-cost labor that causes our inventory to travel so many miles, because each value-added step happens in a different part of the world.

We assume that the way to reduce cost is to move our operations to lower cost regions. This assumption has been true for many years. However, we are starting to see a shift. The dynamic nature of labor markets and the ability to measure true *"landed cost"* are shifting our views on our return on investment. In addition, our goals for optimization are starting to bump into each other as we need to optimize for cost, material security, and carbon emissions – all at the same time.

In a challenge to the assumption that *Centralized is Optimized*, supply chains are starting to explore decentralized operations to bring new capabilities. One example is the Nano Factory from the CPG company Unilever. The Nano Factory fits a full production line inside a 40-foot shipping container. Operated and monitored remotely, it can be moved among the local markets that it serves. Unilever is testing this concept for the flexibility of mobility of decentralizing their operations, rather than using a mega factory that is centrally located.

Using fully burdened, end-to-end costs, what is the real trade-off among cost, emissions, and flexibility that your supply chain makes with a centralized strategy?

ASSUMPTION 2: SUPPLY WILL CONTINUE

Today, we assume we will continue to get supply and that we will have the ability to ship supply to our operations (in our low-cost manufacturing facilities). This assumption has started to unwind and was showcased during the 2020/2021 supply capacity constraints.

There are two points where we can challenge this assumption. The first is at origin and the second is in-transit.

First, we assume that *Supply Will Continue* to come from the planet. This assumption was covered in *Chapter 1* as a consequence of continuing to operate as we do today. You may remember the heat map of the Periodic Table of Elements, showing that several elements have less than 50 years of materials left on the planet. The diminishing supply of primary materials will shift our assumption that *Supply Will Continue.*

Second, we assume that *Supply Will Continue* to make it from the planet all the way to our operations. This last year in 2020, we experienced the challenges of moving supply across borders and keeping inventory on the shelves. Supply, it turns out, will not always be there. An example from 2021 is the silicon chip shortage which has impacts across multiple industries. The issue isn't the raw materials. The issue is everything that happens between the planet and the operations that need to use the chips.

How often does your supply chain struggle to get the supply it needs?

ASSUMPTION 3: WASTE IS THROWN AWAY

The idea that an item can be thrown *"away"* is a great concept to contemplate. In speaking with Tom Raftery from SAP in 2020 on his podcast Digital Supply Chain, he brought up an excellent point. *"Where is away?"* We have this idea that we can dispose of an item or a material and it is no longer a problem.

But these materials are a problem. Sometimes they end up in landfills. And sometimes we – get this – ship our waste from our country to other countries to go into **their** landfills. As a global community, we ship so much garbage to each other that it's called the Global Waste Trade.

Instead, imagine that our supply chains are shorter. The garbage we ship around the world is considered valuable because it contains items and materials that can be used again. *(Did you know that we throw away fully functioning products today?).* So, we stop shipping waste around the world. Instead, the waste produced by our supply chains and cities is captured and used again. This captured waste becomes the source of supply that we will need to operate our supply chains.

The CPG company Procter and Gamble (P&G) was faced with a major challenge. The number of used baby diapers each year tops 20 million tons and nearly a third of the diapers sold worldwide come from P&G. Baby diapers should be thrown away, and it seems impossible that the materials in used baby diapers could add more value to the economy. However, with science, engineering, supply chain, and a joint venture with the Angelini Group called Fater, P&G has launched their first factory in Italy to process dirty diapers. This process uses dirty diapers as in input and produces cellulose, plastic, and absorbent materials at outputs, which can be used again.

What if there was no option to throw materials "away" and instead we were responsible for finding a use for all of the waste produced by our supply chains?

ASSUMPTION 4: WE ARE ON OUR OWN

We have invested a lot of money into our supply chains. We assume that shifting our operations to use shorter supply chains and changing the design of our networks will mean walking away from that investment.

Here are two ideas to challenge this assumption and have our investments still pay returns.

First, it may be that all the infrastructure we use today to run our global supply chains is still needed - it may just not be needed by you. If we consider a shift away from centralized mega factories toward smaller factories located closer to the point of use, we may find ways to reallocate our infrastructure and networks. Better yet, if you have partnered with outsourced service providers then they may be one step ahead of you. Consider asking your Contract Manufacturer about their network flexibility.

Second, consider leveraging infrastructure assistance from the governments where you operate. The Circular Economy is one area where governments around the world are often ahead of corporations. These governments are often eager to partner to support a transition to a circular approach.

Examples include:

- In Kenya, the government is partnering with industry to create closed-loop systems and reduce the level of toxic waste in their supply chains.

- In the U.K., the Waste and Resources Action Program will create 500,000 new jobs, all anchored in circularity.

- In Australia, the Recycling Modernization Fund initiative will divert materials from landfill in an effort to reduce total waste generated and increase material recovery rates for circulation.

- In India, showcase cities like Indore in Madhya Pradesh prove that household collection and waste segregation is possible at scale.

- In Brazil, a new Green Patent Pilot Program has launched to offer a fast-track for patent applications that support green technology, such as the technologies needed to prepare materials for reuse.

What incentive would you need to make a shift in your network design toward a shorter supply chain?

--

In this section, we explored the **processes** of Circular Supply Chains. This section is meant to spark curiosity so you can investigate your own supply chain and explore solutions together with your trading partners. In the next section, we'll turn our attention to the **outputs** of Circular Supply Chains and the transition from producing waste to producing minor value streams.

OUTPUTS OF CIRCULAR SUPPLY CHAINS

Another section means another reminder. Circular Supply Chains are interconnected systems that use secondary and renewable inputs *to generate value* by reducing, then maximizing, resource use. This section explores the outputs we produce in Circular Supply Chains. Circular Supply Chains generate only value. No waste here! Instead, they generate major and minor value streams.

The concepts in both the chapters in this section have been covered previously, so the answers to these two questions will be concise.

10

HOW CAN ANOTHER SUPPLY CHAIN USE MY WASTE?

D o you ever get déjà vu? Like when your sales team comes in and tells you the good news that they have sold inventory that doesn't exist - and then it happens again two months later? Well, you may have the feeling of déjà vu as we answer this question.

This chapter will feel familiar because it is the flip answer of *Chapter 6*. Where *Chapter 6* explored the material relationship from a customer perspective, this chapter explores it from a supplier perspective. In order for you to get Circular Materials from other supply chains as a customer, it means that other supply chains need to make these materials available. Which means that your supply chain – as one of those "other supply chains" will also need to make your materials available. You will become a supplier to new types of customers!

This chapter explores three approaches for how other supply chains can use the waste produced by your supply chain.

APPROACH 1: NEXT DOOR

Other supply chains can use your waste by moving in next door and co-locating their operation with your operation. Consider the concept of industrial symbiosis where multiple production processes cluster together to facilitate an efficient circulation of materials. In these examples, waste has successfully become minor value streams.

An example from the food industry is from a hummus manufacturer. Previously, they discarded millions of pounds of byproduct. After boiling the chickpeas needed for hummus, they disposed of the water used for boiling. Meanwhile, there was a discovery in how to produce vegan mayonnaise using byproduct. (*Sometimes called "aquafaba" because, I suppose, the Italian word sounds better than the English words for "bean water."*) This discovery led the vegan mayonnaise producer to open a factory next door to the hummus factory. The hummus manufacturer stopped worrying about byproduct disposal and instead sold it to their next-door neighbor.

As you consider your minor value streams, it may surprise you that your next customer could move in next door.

APPROACH 2: DOWN THE STREET

Let's imagine there is a direct buyer of your byproduct that is located 200 miles away. While next door is preferred, down the street is still great news. You will not have to pay to dispose of your byproduct and you may even make some money from the sale.

One example of this is from the food producer Heinz. Heinz produces 350 million pounds of ketchup each year, which means that a lot of tomato skins, stems, and seeds are leftover. Down the (figurative) road, an average vehicle produced by Ford requires 300 pounds of plastic. At first this may seem like two completely different topics. But, as it turns out, plastic can be made from nearly any biological material. (*Not just from fossil fuels!*) Heinz and Ford have co-funded bioplastic research to take the byproduct from ketchup manufacturing to create plastic for Ford vehicles.

This type of partnership is also happening with bread for beer, beer for dietary supplements, various types of metals, textiles, e-waste, tires, automotive, and even with prepared food. (*Check out Too Good To Go.*)

Notably, studies on sharing waste among direct partnerships find that we do not have a challenge with finding material candidates for circulation. It is instead the actual coordination of creating bilateral agreements that is causing challenges. If you're keen on this concept, it is worth searching for "eco-industrial parks" in addition to "industrial symbiosis" so you can find examples, benchmarks and others who are also seeking to partner. Be prepared to put forth the leadership to create and manage the partnerships, then relish in the benefits you will get back.

APPROACH 3: WITH SOME HELP

The idea of creating new bilateral agreements may be more time than you can afford to spend right now. If this is the case, then you can call in a broker to take care of your process waste. Now, we've been doing this for years. Scrap metal and pulp, for example, are circulating through our supply chains today.

The industrial waste industry in the USA is valued at nearly $60 billion per year. This will grow and expand as we reconsider waste as secondary value and critical to our supply chains and the global economy. There are already private brokers around the world that exist to connect process waste with material buyers. The options are expanding to include start-ups focused on the Circular Economy. Check out the guidance in your region for more information about selling industrial waste. For example, the US Environmental Protection Agency and the Europe Environmental Agency both have excellent references to use as starting points.

11

ISN'T ZERO WASTE IMPOSSIBLE?

Nope.

Ok you're right, this chapter deserves more attention. For some, "zero waste" falls in the same category as "continuous improvement" meaning that it is a guiding principle for our actions, but a goal we are never meant to achieve. On the other hand, you may already be down the path of zero waste in your own supply chain, or you have interacted with zero-waste processes. This is often clarified as "zero waste to landfill" with the idea that processes will always have a byproduct of some kind, so the goal is to find valuable uses for the byproducts that are produced, rather than throwing them "away."

Let's explore three opportunities that supply chains have to achieve zero waste.

OPPORTUNITY 1: REDUCE THE WASTE

I know what you're thinking. *"We get it, already. Reduce waste. Lean it out."* And you're right. The first principle of the Circular Economy is to design waste out. The best way to reduce waste is to remove the circumstance where the waste was produced.

- Too many emissions from transportation? Shorten the supply chain and remove the transportation.

- Too many quality issues? Remove the troublesome step of the process.

- Too many widgets produced to support a consumer-driven market? Compete with the linear economy with an XaaS offering. This reduces wastes because far fewer items are created to support the same number of customers.

The idea to *Reduce the Waste* may seem simple, and yet - sometimes we forget to consider this because of the assumptions we bring with us as we design, plan, and optimize.

In 2020, I visited the India headquarters of the Kaizen Institute. They applied the idea of reducing waste into their office space. They started with an office space on the top floor of a standard building. They had their sights set on a seemingly impossible goal. With clever design and by working with nature, they turned their top floor office space into India's first LEED Gold certified small office. The natural light is so present they rarely turn on the office lights. The air flow is so well designed they don't need any air conditioning – even in the hottest months in Pune, India. And you should see how they run their office. There are no excess supplies, because everything has a labeled space. (*Literally every pen has a little spot with a little label.*) At the same time every day, a reminder sounds for everyone to pitch in and do office chores for 15 minutes. Even the Managing Director is included. (*When I was there, his chore was to sweep and tidy the outdoor patio.*)

I share this story because it is a reminder to challenge what others see as "impossible." This mindset can apply to our processes and the way we consider the outputs we create. The easiest output to manage is the one we never make.

OPPORTUNITY 2: DIVERT THE WASTE

Now that you have humored me in the previous section that less is always better… the reality check that our processes will create waste is here for this section. Waste diversion is about finding a better use for our materials when compared to landfill. This is all about creating symbiotic relationships with other supply chains who will make use of our process outputs.

There's a fantastic whiskey producer in Seattle called Westland Whiskey. Their goal is to make a name for American Single Malt. (*Please, hold all judgement until you actually try it.*) In the process of making whiskey, the first step is to basically make beer. Then this liquid is distilled. After the "beer making" process, the sugar in the grain has been used to create delicious flavors and alcohol, but still exists as a grain. And, it has nutritional value! Some distilleries throw these grains away. Westland Whiskey, however, sends their spent grains to farms in Washington. This is one example of waste diversion.

Another example comes from the CPG company Procter and Gamble (P&G). (*Yes, them again. Listen, though… they are trying some pretty clever circular ideas!*) The teams sat down and watched their processes when they saw this happen:

- Empty bottles came in from a supplier in cardboard boxes.

- These bottles were removed from the boxes and used as inputs into the filling lines.

- P&G then filled these bottles with their product.

- The filled bottles went into new cardboard boxes.

- These boxes are shipped to retailers.

Do you see the issue?

The boxes.

Supplier packaging was disposed of, new packaging was purchased, and the new packaging was sent on to the customer. To a non-supply-chain-person, this may seem simple. But for us? We know this is difficult to solve. Want to keep the supplier packaging in play? It means refactoring the entire manufacturing line, and P&G did just that.

Today's process looks more like:

- Empty bottles arrive in cardboard boxes.

- The entire box, bottles inside, goes down the manufacturing line.

- The supplier packaging is retained and used to ship to the retailers.

Without question, this took a financial investment from P&G to rebuild and configure their lines. And, they benefit from this change because they no longer dispose of the supplier packaging, they no longer buy new packaging, and they created a new tool on their zero-waste-to-landfill journey.

OPPORTUNITY 3: SELL THE WASTE

We know how to sell our process waste. We have done this for a long time. The goal now is to **sell all the waste.**

In the last chapter, we explored ways to find buyers for your process waste so it can stop being called waste and start being called value instead. As you have already read the basics on this, I'll leave you with several examples instead of telling you the concepts again. Keep this in mind: in a time where *industrial waste* may conjure ideas of sludge and hazardous materials, the reality is most waste we produce can be used by others. (*Of course, the idea is that we first shorten the supply chains and reduce the amount and types of waste produced!*)

- USA-based Mobius anchors in the idea that "There's Wonder in Waste" and has created a business based on buying industrial waste. They take Lignin from paper production, process it to create resins, these resins become other products, and the new products can break down into water and compost. Closed loop!

- The carbon dioxide created during industrial processes can be captured and sold for use in processes such as creating algae and building materials.

- Byproducts from food production such as pineapple tops can be repurposed into textiles.

- Some companies are finding ways to leave items as themselves, creating a shorter circle. Examples include household appliances and consumer electronics. Sometimes these items are never sold in the first place, or they are returned and our supply chains are not equipped to resell them.

- And for something lighthearted, we can turn our attention to an innovation from an arguable start date, in the humble and delicious doughnut hole.

--

This section on *outputs* was a bit of a review as it served as a mirror to the previous section that focused on *inputs*. We looked at approaches to finding buyers for waste and confirmed that it is possible to create zero-waste-to-landfill processes. In the next section, we'll explore the *systems* that surround Circular Supply Chains.

SYSTEMS OF CIRCULAR SUPPLY CHAINS

In this section, we delve into the land of *systems*. I am not a systems design expert, so keep in mind that this section explores systems from a supply chain practitioner's perspective.

As a reminder: Circular Supply Chains *are interconnected systems* that use secondary and renewable inputs to generate value by reducing, then maximizing, resource use. Let's delve into that term *"interconnected system."* This first chapter looks at systems, the next explores what it means to be interconnected, and we close the section with some cool technologies.

12

AREN'T SUPPLY CHAINS ALREADY SYSTEMS?

Supply chains have many trading partners. We know that today's supply chains in the linear economy are not perfect lines between the planet and the customer. Instead, material weaves its way through different nodes and different companies. As our supply chains become more digitized, some folks are now referring to supply chains as "*digital supply networks.*" It's true that supply chains are networks and systems today. And, we have more work to get these systems developed.

To take our supply chain systems to the next level, there will need to be developments made across the industry.

DEVELOPMENT 1: STANDARDS

Have you noticed that different supply chains use slightly different language? We can usually all understand each other, and there are little nuances to what we mean and how we measure the same ideas and concepts. The shared meanings we use are called *Standards*. In the *SCOR Model*, practices are split into emerging, best, and standard. Once a practice is repeatable and shared across the industry, it becomes a standard practice. Examples of which are:

- Emerging practice: 3D Printing
- Best practice: Vendor Managed Inventory
- Standard practice: ABC Inventory Classification

This is important! Imagine if there were no standard sizes for pallets or shipping containers, calculations for inventory holding costs, or Incoterms to guide us when life inevitably happens to our shipments. If we want to dramatically shift our relationship with materials, then standards are an important development for our profession. We will develop new ways to talk about circularity, the concepts we explore, and the new processes we create.

There are standards organizations, like ISO (International Standards Organization in Geneva) or GS1 (out of Brussels). These organizations strive to find common ground across players and industries, so we can have a standard language. Both ISO and GS1 have standards for supply chain and are developing standards around Circular Economy. Neither have standards for Circular Supply Chains. Yet.

Notably: The SCOR model includes a section tucked in the back called "Sustainable SCOR." While they don't use the term "circular," many of the emerging concepts included in the "Sustainable SCOR" section hint at a direction of circularity. There are measures for emissions, renewable energy, water usage, and the percentage of renewable or recyclable materials used in a process. While these measures are high-level today, they point at an encouraging direction for the industry.

DEVELOPMENT 2: MEASURES

The way we measure our supply chains is important. As we walk into new processes, new supply chains, and new regions, one of our first questions as supply chain professionals is "What does good look like?" The answer gives us our direction and mindset for the conversations we have about that supply chain. *Measures* could fall into *Standards*. However, for this chapter I reserve *Standards* to describe processes and allow *Measures* to have their own shining moment.

In 2004, Professor Hau Lee published an article, called "The Triple-A Supply Chain," where he argued that long-lasting supply chain performance anchors in the ability of supply chains to be **agile**, **adaptable**, and **aligned** to the organization they support. All these years later, "The Triple-A Supply Chain," is still frequently referenced among supply chain practitioners.

In addition, Level 1 of the SCOR Model recommends measuring supply chain performance through reliability, responsiveness, agility, cost, and return on assets.

And often, I simplify supply chain measurements down three measures: Time, cost, and quality.

These three examples of different ways to measure show that even with today's linear supply chains, "good" is not consistent. We should be cheaper (*unless we shouldn't*), faster (*except when we choose not to be*) and have great quality (*but only if that's the strategy*). As we transition to circularity, how do we draw a line in the sand to use as a benchmark for performance? We use tomorrow's measures.

In tomorrow's measures, circularity is a strategy, not a goal.

In tomorrow's measures, circularity is a strategy, not a goal. I predict that our Level 1 performance goals (cost, agility, reliability, and so forth) will remain the same, and our Level 2 Measures will expand to include circularity measures. Together, we will develop what it means to measure a Circular Supply Chain so that we know if we are improving. And it is important that we develop common Measures so that different trading partners are using the same guidance for performance.

Coming up, *Chapter 14* explores technology and data, and *Chapter 16* offers a few measures as starting points.

DEVELOPMENT 3: MODULARITY

Once upon a time, in the supply chain industry 20 years ago, there was a concept called Turnkey Vendors. The idea was to access various outsourced functions for the supply chain "with the turn of a key," meaning to easily pop-up and pop-down various operations. While the term "Turnkey" has lost favor over the years, the concept continues to be present through our supply chains.

The flexibility that *Modularity* could offer us is outstanding. The reality is that we often create our processes in a way that works well for our supply chains, but are not common across supply chains. This means that we usually get involved in how our outsourced partners do their tasks for our supply chains, and they end up as more of an extension of our supply chain rather than a functionality that can be turned on or off. The upside of this is the deep relationships that make our supply chains function today. The downside is that we do not have access to the flexibility that these providers could offer.

As we transition from linear to circular, we will experiment and learn and improve. The options we have for outsourced services will expand and allow us to shorten our supply chains and circulate materials. Modularity is critical for us to access the capabilities that we want, such as:

- (Re)manufacture closer to customers

- Balance new builds and repairs

- Source a variety of Circular Materials from a variety of sources

- Increase utilization of the assets in our value chains

- Scale up and down with seasonality

- Shorten supply chains and reduce emissions

The development of modular capabilities will have an impact on the touchpoints we have with our trading partners. Let's explore these touchpoints in the next chapter.

13

WHAT DOES IT MEAN TO BE INTERCONNECTED?

W e're connected to our trading partners today, but we are rarely *inter*connected. Am I splitting hairs? Maybe. And yet, over the next several paragraphs you will see why these are hairs worth splitting.

In a Circular Supply Chain, every operation is the source of raw materials for another operation. We will lean on each other more than we do today, and we'll become suppliers to new types of customers – and customers to new types of suppliers.

Becoming more interconnected than we are today means having more touchpoints across our networks. If we want to move from connected to interconnected, we will become more reliant and dependent on our trading partners. Consider an ecosystem in nature, where removing one component can collapse the ecosystem.

TOUCHPOINT 1: PHYSICAL

If you have read even half the chapters leading up to this one, this first touchpoint will be super familiar. In a Circular Supply Chain, we circulate materials among supply chains and users. These materials are one of the touchpoints that runs among our supply chains.

As Circular Materials enter our Circular Supply Chains, they come from secondary or renewable sources. If it is from a secondary source, it has been used before and it is coming from a user or from a supply chain. If it is renewable, it comes from the planet or from biology and grows back. We take these materials into our supply chains and use them in a way that reduces the amount we need and ensures the longest lifecycle possible. As the material comes out of our process, it goes to the major customer of the process or the minor customer of the process.

Still with me? (*Don't yawn, this is just a touch of review.*)

Now, let's apply to a few business models and test if our operations are circular:

- Traditional product sale: Our company sells pumps to supply chains to be used in their manufacturing facility. To facilitate a Circular Operation, our supply chains sources Circular Materials such as previously used pumps, spare parts, and secondary metals. There is a touchpoint with our suppliers.

- XaaS: Our company sells the value of a pump to supply chains. We monitor the performance of the pump, and performance maintenance required. To facilitate a Circular

Operation, our supply chain sources Circular Materials for use in the maintenance process. This includes lubricants, spare parts, and the transportation for the engineer traveling to the site.

• Reuse models: Our company sells industrial packaging that pumps are shipped in. It is robust and reusable. To facilitate a Circular Operation, our supply chain tracks this packaging as assets. The use of sensors allows us to manage this physical touchpoint with our customers.

The physical touchpoints in supply chains are usually the easiest to identify. Let's move on to the less tangible touchpoints: Financial and information.

TOUCHPOINT 2: FINANCIAL

Early in my career, I was a supply chain data and process analyst. It was awesome. In the pursuit of continuous improvement, I quickly learned that the narrative from different supply chain stakeholders varied and often did not tell me the "whole truth" about what decisions had been made. Instead, I turned to a different type of truth: Money.

While financial flows do not follow physical flows, they often tell us more about our inventory than the inventory does! Financial touchpoints show us decision makers and decision timing. We can see business rules and contract terms. We can see when we have quality issues and when the process did not go to plan. (*Hello, expedites!*)

In the interconnected system of Circular Supply Chains, the financial relationships we have with our trading partners will expand past what we have today. The financial touch points we have will become easier to set up and shut down, so we can support the modular approach that we will take in the near future to have access to the materials we need. Imagine that our inputs will vary from a single material today and expand to include a variety of materials, WIP, and finished goods. And we will get these items from a variety of stakeholders.

Financial touchpoints with suppliers are complemented with financial touchpoints with financing bodies. Financing for circularity is on the rise: Private equity, private market funds, and outstanding corporate bonds with a focus on the Circular Economy are quickly emerging around the world from companies like BlackRock, Goldman Sachs, Alphabet, Henkel and Philips. The Ellen MacArthur Foundation finds that private equity funds with at least a partial focus on the Circular Economy outperform other funds.

As financing increases for our focus on Circular Supply Chains, so will the financial transactions we have with our trading partners. Will it be worth it to stand up and shut down different contracts with individual partners? I don't think so.

A small side bar. It may be shocking that it's taken me 13 chapters to use the word *blockchain* so here it is: blockchain. At Circular Economy conferences over these last few years, I have eagerly attended sessions that promise to explore Circular Economy for supply chain and the importance of traceability for successful circular models. These sessions focused on the use of blockchain as a brilliant solution to our supply chain woes.

The issue with this, of course, is the tremendous amount of work we need to do in process, standards, measurement systems and partner contracts – before we can effectively use enabling technologies like blockchain. The use of blockchain is often recommended without acknowledging the prerequisites required for the blockchain solution to deliver its intent.

While I don't think blockchain in its current form will be the long-term solution for our supply chains given the high amount of energy it requires, there are a few use cases where I see blockchain as the only option we have today. Here comes the first use case I begrudgingly accept as a use case for blockchain.

Now, back to our regularly scheduled program. Here is my over-simplified version of why it matters for supply chain:

> *1.* Data is hashed so that humans can't read it. *(Hashing means that human-readable data is translated into a series of characters. That series of characters, the hash, is then used to represent the original data. Only those with the "key" will be able to turn these hashes back into human-readable data. In this way, we can share data about our processes that would otherwise make us squeamish.)*

> 2. There is a chain of custody for the product, the data, and the finances that can't be changed or re-written.

> 3. Business rules can be set up to be automatically executed. When a shipment is received and the paperwork matches, payment can be released.

This is how we would use a blockchain capability: Imagine we need a material. We can search for it in a nearby marketplace that connects us directly to sellers. We find the material we need from a seller we have never worked with before. Instead of taking several weeks to establish a contract and payment terms, we leverage a template contract that has been created specifically to leverage blockchain.

This may not seem revolutionary for your supply chain. If that's the case, congrats – your supply chain is ahead of the rest. For most of us, the ability to exchange financials easily is a big deal. We will cover another blockchain use case in this next chapter as we explore technology.

Regardless of where your supply chain is on the financial wizardry journey, your financials will change in the coming years.

TOUCHPOINT 3: INFORMATION

If you thought financials were interesting, wait till you hear about the data.

Ten years ago, I was managing a launch. It was 9pm and I was still in my office. We had one final case of launch product to ship out of the warehouse. It had arrived, physically, to the warehouse. The driver was ready to leave. But we were all just waiting, because our ERP system hadn't finished recognizing the inventory. So we all just hung out on a conference call (*those old contraptions where we had bridge numbers that we typed into the phone*) until **ding!** there it was in the system, and I could drop the order for the warehouse to process and release the inventory.

If inventory flows are the castle, then information flows are the drawbridge (*and financials are the moat*). We can forget the drawbridge exists until it goes up, and then everything else around it stops.

If inventory flows are the castle, then information flows are the drawbridge (and financials are the moat).

The information flows in our supply chains are one of the coolest and strangest showcases of creativity I've ever seen. Have you had the honor of being in a white boarding session with a zillion sticky notes all around, and as you unwind the information flows around your supply chain – and see the faces of your peers as their eyes widen, mouths drop, and we all realize... *"We do what?"* (You know how this plays out, right? *"Yes, yes, we did that. Remember during our last ERP upgrade and we "improved" the process? This was such a great work-around! We were all so proud."*)

The mazes we create are truly impressive. Now imagine our information flows *(with the imperfect master data, incomplete fields, fat-fingered values, and short-hand-that-only-Nancy-understands)* get a major steroid injection that's called the Circular Supply Chain. We have more information, more scenarios, and different dynamic tolerance ranges. Buckle up!

14

WHAT ABOUT TECHNOLOGY?

There is a great debate on our horizon.

There are opinions about the next industrial revolution. We are currently not yet through the fourth industrial revolution, and we're already talking about the fifth!

As the world's quickest review of the industrial revolutions:

1. 250 years ago, the first industrial revolution began and brought us the power of steam and machines.

2. 100 years later, the second industrial revolution brought us electricity and mass production.

3. 100 years after that (*now we're in the 1970s*), the third industrial revolution happened. This one doesn't get much press, but it was all about robotics and automation.

4. Now just 50 years later, we're in the middle of the fourth industrial revolution.

In the fourth industrial revolution, the sophistication of technology is as high as it has ever been. The cost of digitizing our supply chains, like adding sensors to hardware, is the lowest it has ever been. We have more data than we have ever had, and we are developing a smart, connected world. We are exploring concepts like lights-out manufacturing and self-driving supply chains.

Here's where the first debate comes in. We are *already* talking about the *next* industrial revolution. Some big thinkers claim that the fifth industrial revolution will be about hyper-individualization in the form of Lot Size 1. Some claim that it will be focused on co-bots: how humans and machines work together.

I claim that we aren't even through the fourth industrial revolution yet, so it seems premature to work on the fifth.

This is my prediction:

• The fourth industrial revolution will mature to showcase that our smart, connected world exists so that we can take better care of our materials. We will progress into Lot Size 1 *because we can, it's needed, and there's no reason to wait.*

However, "Lot Size 1" can have different definitions. We'll cover that in this chapter.

• The fifth industrial revolution will be a *Green Revolution*, purely out of dire need. It doesn't matter who "wants" to have it as a focus. It will happen. We are running out of materials and, while we are *very talented* as a profession, even we cannot source materials that do not exist.

- There will be zero years between the fourth and fifth industrial revolutions.

The first debate is about what we're getting out of the fourth industrial revolution. The second debate is about "lights-out manufacturing," a concept that means we can run our processes without the lights on, because it is fully automated. No people in the process means no lights are needed. On the other hand, what happens if we need to repair and remanufacture? We haven't trained robots – yet – to do the skilled labor needed to diagnose and repair. For this, we need the lights on. What a great tension to hold.

Technology is always fun to explore, and what I've learned from years of successful - and failed - IT projects is that without a cool code name, the project doesn't have a chance at succeeding. No one will come to meetings. So, the sections in this chapter are named with cool code names, because we're on Chapter 14 and you're so close to finishing out this journey with me.

Look, most of our supply chains need a lot of work in the technology area. We're on our way toward digitization, but we aren't at the finish line yet. Our processes are complex, the landscapes we operate in are bonkers, and we're all crazy busy. But change is coming. Let's go over five technologies that are worth a moment of contemplation to help us during this change.

TECHNOLOGY 1: PANORAMA

We need to see our supply chains. We need to see what comes in, what goes out, material origins, byproduct destinations, batch numbers, repair needs, risk profiles, and so on. Without a foundation of digitization, we will struggle to go circular. Anchoring a digital transformation in a purpose like circularity gives our teams a goal they care about and decision criteria to use when making design decisions.

At the same time, we need to prioritize the data that we decide to gather and store. Digital waste is real, and it is growing. The guidance here is to be selective and intentional with your digitization efforts.

As early as 2011, a couple of Johns Hopkins researchers explored the concept of digital waste. They developed four categories:

1. Unintentional waste data, created as a byproduct of a process, with no purpose.

2. Used data, which has served its purposes and is no longer useful.

3. Degraded data, also known as data rot, which cannot be used any more.

4. Unwanted data, which was never useful in the first place.

Consider the potential for digital waste in your supply chain: order data, master data, simple math, fancy math. We already use a lot of data today.

The goal of Panorama is to help you see what you need to see, to tackle the initiatives you have coming in the next two years.

Are you digitized enough to accomplish what you need?

Panorama is the code name for this section because this is about digitization, and digitization allows us to see a panoramic view of our supply chains.

TECHNOLOGY 2: SNOWFLAKE

Let's talk Lot Size 1. Some claim this will be the focus of the fifth industrial revolution. The reality is, we're already dipping our toes in the water. Lot Size 1 is the idea that we'll get to hyper-individualization. This is a concept with early traction among the medical community to create medical care for a specific human. This idea is gaining popularity and we're seeing quasi-individualization in different industries, such as clothing where items are laser cut to order based on customized measurements.

Now consider Lot Size 1 in terms of the idea for a Digital Bill of Materials (BOM). A Digital BOM will be a digital companion of a physical good and tell the supply chain important information about that material. This is the second use case for blockchain that I'll cover in this book.

Sharing everything we know about a product is not something we want to do lightly. This Digital BOM will contain information about materials, origin, utilities, repair, quality, and so forth. This is information that should only be shared with certain stakeholders. As materials circulate and are used again, we also need to know their life stories. For example, we need to know if the item is safe for human use. This makes the Digital BOM a good candidate for blockchain, because (1) the data needs to be hashed, and (2) the chain of custody is important.

A Digital BOM can be used in a few helpful ways:

- Repair: The history of the product including use, material types, and self-diagnostics to accelerate the repair and improve the quality.

- Circular Materials: Information about that material and its origin.

- Circular Operations: Additional inputs other than materials and their origins, such as water and electricity.

- Stakeholder information: Both consumers and trading partners have interest in the digital identity of our products.

The idea of a Digital BOM is similar to the idea of a Digital Thread, which acts as a record of an item through its life.

How close are you to creating a Digital BOM?

Snowflake is the code name for this section because this is about the unique nature of individual assets and equipment. As we use and reuse, our items become unique and special.

TECHNOLOGY 3: LEGO

LEGO is about modularity. In Chapter 12 we explored developing modularity as an industry, and in Chapter 13 we looked at the touchpoints needed. This section gives a nod to the technologies that support modularity.

Creating technology connections with our partners has come a long way. It used to take months to establish a single message exchange with a trading partner. But the digital connections we make still take more time and effort than they should.

Circular Supply Chains are flexible in the materials and partners they use. Imagine the data connections needed to support identifying and sourcing a variety of Circular Materials as inputs to our processes and communicating and selling a variety of Circular Materials as outputs from our processes.

The difficulty in creating these modular technology connections often comes because we do not use the same standards. While *Standards* may seem like a boring topic, they actually become the foundation for us to go circular together. Data connections in our linear supply chains are already difficult, and the amount of data we will add in Circular Supply Chains means that the role of standards becomes even more important. There are industry groups, like the Capital Equipment Coalition hosted by PACE (Platform to Accelerate the Circular Economy), that pulls together industries in a pre-competitive space to begin creating these standards.

How long does it take your supply chain to connect with a new trading partner?

LEGO is the code name for this section because... you guessed it... this is about snap in, snap out. Consequently, LEGO as a company is also taking pretty tremendous approaches to circularity.

TECHNOLOGY 4: ULTRA

When I worked in the digital arm at GE building industrial software, one of our customers called and asked for help with something really cool. They basically described industrial symbiosis: How do I take a byproduct from one factory and send it to another automatically? This, to me, is one of the coolest planning and execution problems ever.

Imagine an ecosystem like industrial symbiosis and expand it to be dynamic and geographically spread out. Every day, materials from each operation are optimized for exchange with other operations. It's like a miniature commodities exchange market happening all day, every day. The amount of data needed about each operation (digital twin), tolerance range for materials (target Digital BOM), acceptance criteria for Circular Materials, timing, quality... then to execute against it – and to have all of this happen between organizations *is so cool*.

Imagine that idea of a self-driving supply chain. While there is a tension with repair and remanufacturing, there are elements of the supply chain that could self-drive. The idea that cross-organization execution could happen fully automated is both thrilling and somehow terrifying, given the state of today's data connections.

I've been told that I think too far out into the future. But to me, Circular Supply Chains are not a future problem. We need to create systems to support relationships that aren't created, materials that haven't been invented, physical flows that aren't possible, and performance metrics we haven't defined. All while our process inputs are at risk. Software takes a long time to develop, so to me, this is a today-right now-what-are-we-waiting-for problem.

This section embraces the idea of Cross-Enterprise Planning and Execution, but that sounds mundane, hence the code name.

If you could pick one supplier and one customer to be connected to for next-level planning and execution, who would they be?

Ultra is the code name for this section because an ultra-marathon is a long distance and with the proper type of cross-enterprise systems in place, we can see our operations remotely – from a long distance.

TECHNOLOGY 5: VEGAS

Running simulations and "what-if" scenarios is an imperfect science for many of our supply chains. The environments we operate in are so complex that our models often capture only part of the variables as play. And this is fine for the most part. We only need so much data to answer the questions we have today.

As we transition into Circular Supply Chains, we'll have new questions and new scenarios to run. Consider the below examples. Could you answer these today?

- Where on the planet do my materials start from today?

- Is it possible to change my sourcing strategy to include materials from only within 500 miles?

- If I change my sourcing strategy, can I still meet my performance targets?

- If I decentralize manufacturing, where would I put the new factories?

- Which of my minor value streams are most valuable to which markets?

When considering your supply chain as a Circular Supply Chain, what scenario would you want to run first?

Vegas is the code name for this section because anything is possible in Las Vegas. What happens in a simulation stays in the simulation. Except when we recommend it to the big boss. Then all bets are off.

--

This section focused on the **systems** of Circular Supply Chains and has explored how Circular Supply Chains will move away from silos of protected information and into an approach that enables data sharing in a way where parties feel safe and critical information about circulating materials can be exchanged.

Taking the Next Step Toward Circular Supply Chains

Congratulations! You have arrived at the final section of this book. In it, we'll catapult ourselves into a Circular Supply Chain and find ways to start transitioning our supply chains from linear to circular.

15

WHAT IS THE FUTURE OF SUPPLY CHAINS?

Future-facing articles about supply chains imagine innovative uses of emerging technologies, full automation including autonomous vehicles, and blockchain. In this section, let's imagine realistic scenarios that we face today and will continue to face in the coming years.

Let's look at five scenarios for the future of supply chain. Four will be realistic scenarios, answered by Circular Supply Chain strategies. The last one will be a bit more fun.

SCENARIO 1: YOUR BUDGET IS NO LONGER

Think back to the last time you were asked to reduce your cost per unit, quarter spend, or overall budget. This happens to us a lot, and for good reason. One of the major value-adds we bring to organizations is to optimize for cost. At the same time, the "race to zero" is unsustainable and we need to find new tools to help us.

But have no fear! In these five scenarios, we are in a Circular Supply Chain, and we have options. In this scenario, your budget has been cut so you go and find what can be done, such as:

- Operational Expenses (OpEx) will come down because you've found a secondary source of materials for your largest process input. You've joined a buying group to drive market prices down, saving even more.

- OpEx comes down more because you've found a way to reduce the energy bill in your factories by 30% by changing the process, and by switching to renewable energy sources.

- OpEx comes once again because you've found a buyer for your largest minor value stream produced in your operations, so you can avoid the disposal fee and gain a new revenue source.

- Capital Expenses (CapEx) will go down because you'll have a better handle on how to make the assets in your operations last longer by stretching their lifecycle.

When we are faced with budget cuts in a linear supply chain, we often turn to outsourcing to low-cost labor markets. However, circularity offers us new options.

SCENARIO 2: SUPPLY IS NOT AVAILABLE

Sometime in the 2020-2021 timeframe, you, your suppliers, or customers likely experienced a supply shortage. This could have happened for many reasons and will continue to happen in the future.

In a Circular Supply Chain, you have new options for this scenario. You dramatically reduce your reliance on primary raw materials. By sourcing Circular Materials instead, you are able to decouple the amount of primary materials you need to support more growth in the business. For example, your supply chain is:

- A flexible operation that can take different material quality and variations, so you have more options to keep the operation running when your Plan A, Plan B, and Plan C all fall short.

- Sharing water with nearby factories, reducing the amount of water needed as an input.

- Launching a take-back program so your supply chain can remanufacture in addition to making new items.

- Part of a pilot program to test an electric fleet to eliminate your dependency on traditional vehicle fuel.

By leveraging Circular Materials as process inputs, the supply chain can mitigate challenges in getting supply.

SCENARIO 3: STUCK AT PORT

Now let's imagine supply is available and on the way to our operations. However, it needs to clear a port and sometimes shipments are stuck at the port for various reasons. Inevitably, this happens during a launch or other critical time in your operations.

Circular Supply Chains source regionally which reduces the impact of port closures. For example:

- Partnering with local metal brokers to source the metals most important to the operation.

- Switching from traditional plastics to using bioplastic made from regionally sourced bio scraps that are processed nearby.

- Decentralizing factory operations to be closer to the point of material inputs and outputs, like the Nano Factory from Unilever.

In the future of supply chain, decentralized operations will become more common.

SCENARIO 4: VOLUNTOLD INTO EMISSIONS TARGET

Have you ever been "voluntold" to do something? It's like volunteering, only you didn't volunteer, you were told to do it. Voluntold.

One day, I walked into work and my boss asked if I had seen the company's new announcement that morning. I had. She responded, "Great, that's now your job." Sometimes we find out about our responsibilities after they have been announced!

You may have recently been voluntold about a carbon emissions target, which may have come with mixed emotions. On the one hand, you're excited that your company has made a commitment. On the other, you aren't sure how you'll pull it off.

And then you remember you run a Circular Supply Chain and you have options. Such as:

- Transportation accounts for 15% of global emissions. Your strategy of a short, regional supply chain and electric fleet dramatically reduces your carbon output.

- Because your supply chain is local, you have nearly eliminated the need for air freight, which is a huge carbon emitter.

- Energy is about a third of carbon emissions worldwide. Because of this, you reduce the energy use in your operations, and switch to renewable sources of energy.

- You take a critical look at the AI you use in your supply chain. Training an off-the-shelf AI language-processing system produces a lot of emissions. (There is tremendous debate over how much, exactly. Research this and decide for yourself.) Using AI responsibly and choosing a cloud provider with a circular strategy helps you get closer to your emissions goals.

I have spoken with many senior supply chain leaders around the world that find themselves in this position. The curiosity about circularity is growing as one way to help tackle emissions.

SCENARIO 5: A BOLDER LOOK

The first four scenarios are reasonable. While circularity in our supply chains is still a future aspiration for some, we can imagine these scenarios playing out. Now let's go bolder with two future statements related to Circular Supply Chains.

First, the future of supply chain is on-demand. We will have access to more supply chain functionalities around the world, while owning less than we do today.

Today, we send our production orders to our factories. Even if we don't own them, the factories we use often work as an extension of our supply chains. We complete network design and cost optimizations to figure out where these factories should be located.

In the future, imagine a network of manufacturers around the world. Imagine that just as you can drop an order to a logistics network today, you can drop a production order to a manufacturing network. The order management and routing will send the order you dropped to the factory closest to the customer. These factories will produce goods for different companies – on the same line. Lot sizes will get smaller. On-demand supply chains keep utilization of our assets high and allows us to build only what is needed and where it is needed.

Second, the future of supply chain is *less complex*. Yes, circularity adds complexity in some ways. But it reduces complexity in others. Let's go back to the idea of Lot Size 1. Additive manufacturing or 3D printing can reduce the complexity of our supply chains. GE Aviation has created solutions that redefines how to build an item with additive manufacturing. The innovation reduces the number of suppliers from 50 down to one, and 300 component parts down to one. The shift from managing 50 suppliers or 300 SKUs down to just one is dramatic. Additive manufacturing is one technology that will support hyper-individualization. It reduces the number of components that are needed which means fewer materials coming from future origins. It designs waste out!

--

Will these future states happen? We'll find out together. Let's imagine a future with less complexity, and all the effort and math we're using today can go toward something that truly matters.

16

How do linear supply chains become circular?

The most common question I am asked about Circular Supply Chains is what supply chains can do today to get started in the transition from linear to circular. My answer is to describe the first phase of this chapter.

This chapter outlines seven phases I originally developed for an article I wrote for the *Journal of Supply Chain Management, Logistics and Procurement* called *Supplying the Circular Economy*. These seven phases are used at the Circular Supply Chain Network as the basis of their Transition Framework to provide a shared language to have global conversations about Circular Supply Chains.

These may not be the "right" phases or what we'll end up calling each of these phases in the future. The phases are meant to provide language and structure so we can get going on our transitions from linear to circular. The terms I use in these phases expand on the common language used in the circularity community.

One of my favorite phrases is that in a Circular Supply Chain, "Everything is Inventory!" I even have a sweatshirt with this across the front. The way inventory flows through our supply chains is fascinating! As we explore these seven phases, we'll imagine the world as inventory. I use the term "inventory" broadly here to include materials, consumables, assets, and items.

Measurements for the phases described below are suggested and the target for all the measures shared is 100%.

PHASE 1: IDENTIFY INVENTORY

Before we make any changes to our processes, we need to find out what we're doing today. Every time we look at our processes, we do it with a different lens. Using a circularity lens, we look for today's waste streams that can be eliminated or can become tomorrow's value streams.

In the *Identify Inventory* phase, we return to the idea of the value stream map (VSM). The inventory we aim to identify are the materials that never make it into our VSMs. Consider the materials that we don't directly pay for, such as supplier packaging. We can miss these in our VSMs because they don't have a direct impact on our finances.

Bill McDonough of the Cradle to Cradle Institute has a way to talk about carbon emissions. He calls it "fugitive carbon" because the carbon has escaped and is out where we don't want it to be. I use this concept and apply it to value. Our processes today have fugitive value, because materials escape our value streams, and we don't know where the materials are. Today we call those materials pollution and waste. But in a Circular Economy, every material has value. Our goal is to make sure that every material is adding the most value it can.

As you look at your processes, note what comes in and goes out – by weight. Everything can be measured: Metal, plastic, water, air, steam, and consumables. For each process, you will get two numbers: An input and an output. These two numbers will be by material, by process step, in aggregate or in detail. Then compare these numbers and see how far apart they are. For example, perhaps your process uses 500 kg of material as inputs, and you can measure 400 kg as output. There is a gap here and value is becoming fugitive because we can't measure it, or it becomes a waste stream. The goal of this step is to:

1. Learn where your inputs come from

2. Where your outputs go

3. The gap in measurement between input and output

As with any process change or improvement initiative, measuring the current state is the first step. This phase is about awareness and spotting the potential for new value streams.

PHASE 2: INTENSIFY INVENTORY

As a reminder, the first principle of the Circular Economy is to design waste out, and the second principle is to keep materials in use. This second phase uses both of these principles.

After we identify the inventory that may be fugitive or linear, the goal is to increase utilization of inventory in a process. In the circularity community, this is called intensifying use. The more a material is used, the more value it adds to the economy.

We can *Intensify Inventory* in three ways:

1. Redesign business models, such as Product-as-a-Service.

2. Redesign products to be modular, so individual parts can be swapped and repaired, allowing the product to continue being used even as one component is repaired.

3. Redesign the process. This is what we own in supply chain.

Business model and product redesign will have impacts on the supply chain, so inquire across your organization about plans for either. We own the process, so we have more influence over potential process redesign decisions. During a process redesign, look for ways to shorten your supply chain and increase utilization of the equipment and assets throughout the process.

Make note of often each piece of equipment is used through the processes that you own.

PHASE 3: NARROW INVENTORY

Once the supply chain is shorter, the focus becomes leaning out and using less. We covered this idea in *Chapter 8,* so I'll keep this short.

The idea is to eliminate waste. As we explored in *Chapter 11,* there are three approaches to take to eliminate waste. First, we reduce, then we divert, and then we sell. In this way, we reduce the amount produced as a byproduct and then we transform waste into value.

Measuring this phase is done by measuring how much waste is eliminated across these three approaches.

PHASE 4: PREDICT INVENTORY

In *Chapter 14,* we explored technology and the fourth industrial revolution that brings us into a smart, connected world. With digitization and math, our equipment is smarter and our processes are becoming smarter, too. We have more visibility to what travels through our processes today than we ever have.

The focus of this phase is to predict the inventory throughout our operations. We focus on both major and minor value streams. Depending on your digitization journey, the minor value stream may be a challenge. We don't like to talk about how much waste we produce and we have not traditionally prioritized finding "fugitive value." If you are aiming to reduce your emissions, then the *Predict Inventory* phase will work in your favor.

This phase allows us to make better decisions in the following phases. We aim to predict:

- Machine use, wear, and tear. Predict MRO requirements so we can be ready and keep the machine in use as long as possible.

- Major value streams, including WIP and finished goods. (You probably already do this today.)

- Minor value streams, so we can reduce, divert, and sell it.

Measuring this phase is done by looking at "forecast accuracy." I use quotes here because for some of us, it will expand the traditional use of forecasting beyond major value streams.

PHASE 5: SLOW INVENTORY

The goal of this phase is to leave an item as itself for as long as possible. To achieve this, companies are looking at their business models and designers are redesigning. In supply chain, we can achieve this through inventory, equipment, and process.

This phase takes the prediction from *Phase 4: Predict Inventory* and makes it a reality. We covered the different ways to make inventory last in *Chapter 5* when we explored Circular Materials. Remember to keep the circle as small as possible, for as long as possible. The smaller the circle, the less we need to do to the item.

Imagine each version of a product could last twice as long as the version before it. Look around you and imagine that could be true for everything you see. Now imagine it for your supply chain. This is the direction we are heading as we shift from an economy based on planned obsolescence to one based on valuing materials.

Looking internally at your supply chain operations, measure this phase by how long the equipment in your supply chain lasts. Looking externally at the value you offer to customers, partner across your organization to ask: *"What would it take for the product we sell to last twice as long?"* It may not be a popular question, and it will certainly start a series of interesting discussions.

PHASE 6: CLOSE INVENTORY

Closing the loop is perhaps the most common theme across circularity discussions. The focus tends to be in two areas. First, finding uses for waste like plastic. Second, for companies to get their own products back again.

These two focuses are certainly valid. And, there are additional ways to consider closing the loop in the *Close Inventory* phase. Again, we want to keep the smallest circles possible for as long as possible, like we explored in *Chapter 5*. The goal of this phase is to make sure we have material circles established in our supply chains. This might look like:

- Using refurbished spare parts

- Repairing and remanufacturing products to be sold again

- Using Circular Materials for production, including consumables, renewable energy, and biomaterials

I predict that certain elements of our products will become standardized across organizations so that we can share more and collectively repair more effectively. As more items become standard through our supply chains, we can share more among supply chains. Some examples may include industrial packaging, flow spare parts, or components used in consumer electronics.

Measuring this is looking at process inputs to see how much comes from primary materials, and how much comes from Circular Materials.

PHASE 7: CAPTURE INVENTORY

This phase is called *Capture Inventory,* in recognition of the growing industry around taking the fugitive value that is out in the world and preparing it to have another life. Consider the concept of ocean plastics in leggings, sneakers, or plastic laundry detergent bottles. The brand creating these items is not the same company as the one taking the plastic out of the ocean and processing it to be used again.

For the foreseeable future, we will be capturing inventory out of the environment. Because we use so much material each year and reuse so little of it, there is a lot of material hanging out in oceans, in landfills, and the environment.

I predict this industry will grow rapidly in the coming decade as we recognize the importance of using the material that we have already mined or otherwise taken from the planet.

The target for the measures for all of these phases is 100%. The measures of the first six phases start at 0% and our goal is to work up to 100%. However, with this *Capture Inventory* phase, our starting point is greater than 100%. Today, we take materials from the planet. We take as much as we can, and we push it into the economy. Then we find uses for it. Today we take more than what we need. We measure this phase by *Capacity* and the goal is to take only what we need to support our supply chains. Our goal is to come down to 100%.

SUMMARY OF PHASES

To summarize this chapter, check out the table below:

Phase	Focus	Measure
Identify Inventory	Identify circular potential	In:Out Ratio
Intensify Inventory	Shorten supply chain and increase equipment use	Utilization
Narrow Inventory	Lean, Kaizen	Waste Elimination
Predict Inventory	Forecast major and minor value streams	"Forecast Accuracy"
Slow Inventory	Extend the life of a product	Version Improvement
Close Inventory	Use again	Circular Inputs
Capture Inventory	Prepare materials for reuse	Capacity

17

HOW DO I TAKE THE NEXT STEP?

W e've spent this whole book laying the foundation of the questions that need to be answered so you can take the next step toward a Circular Supply Chain. Now, I leave you with five actionable questions to ask your own teams, your own executives, and your own peers. When asking these questions, you'll be in a tremendous position to accelerate your circular journey.

QUESTION 1: WHAT ARE THE MATERIALS WE USE MOST, AND WHERE DO THEY COME FROM?

Depending on how many miles materials travel before they get to your operations, it is surprisingly difficult to figure out where those materials come from. By answering this question, you will begin to view your supply chain through a circular lens. The result of answering this question will show you how much primary and secondary material you use. The answer will put you in a position to know materials types and quantities that need to shift from a linear material to a Circular Material.

Start this investigation with your largest purchases, your friendliest supplier, a controversial material – any criteria will work to get started. The first step is always the most difficult, if these are new questions for your operation.

QUESTION 2: HOW FAR DOES OUR MOST POPULAR PRODUCT TRAVEL?

This can be a fun experience for your team. Choose the product that you sell the most of and attempt to map the complete travel of each of the components. Again, this will be a challenge as we'll often run into answers such as *"it depends."* Does your product travel farther than a pepper grinder?

Answering this question will create a starting point for measuring your journey to a shorter supply chain.

QUESTION 3: WHAT BYPRODUCT DO WE PRODUCE THE MOST OF, AND WHERE?

Question 1 focused on inputs and Question 2 focused on end-to-end travel. This question explores the byproduct, or minor value streams. By answering this question, you will identify an area of potential revenue.

A next-level variation of Question 2 is to include the answer of Question 3. This is to say: Do we include the miles traveled by byproducts in the total miles traveled by a product? If the byproduct of your supply chain is getting shipped to another country for disposal, how will you capture this? I recommend using a *"full burdened"* view as a starting point and including *Byproduct Miles* as a secondary measure to *Total Miles*.

QUESTION 4: WHERE ARE WE MOST VULNERABLE?

Circularity can be a risk mitigator for your supply chain. As we discussed earlier, shorter supply chains offer fewer opportunities for risk to pop up and disrupt your operations.

Answer this question as it relates to your most important performance metric. If time (service level) is your most important performance metric, find a point in your supply chain that leaves you vulnerable.

By answering this question, you set the stage to mitigate this step with a circular strategy.

QUESTION 5: WHAT ARE OUR EMISSIONS LEVELS FOR THE LAST FIVE YEARS?

Many companies are now setting emissions targets for 2030 and stepping-stone targets for 2025. Supply chains play a critical role in achieving these targets. Some analysts estimate that supply chains contribute as much as 90% of a company's carbon emissions.

By answering this question, you will have a view into current emissions and if you are trending up or down. You will also discover your largest areas of emissions which will assist you in creating an action plan to reduce them.

--

For the very final reminder: Circular Supply Chains are interconnected systems that use secondary and renewable inputs to generate value by reducing, then maximizing, resource use. This should all feel quite familiar to you by now.

AS WE FINISH OUR DRINKS...

Some of the ideas explored in this book seem a little futuristic and that's because, in some cases, they are *just ideas*. They'll continue to be ideas until a supply chain professional like you takes them and develops them into proof of concepts, proof of values, pilots, and then into scalable, operational reality.

As a supply chain professional, the decisions you make are powerful. They determine the future of our industry, our economies, and our planet. In this way, Circular Supply Chains will happen when we decide they should. Your decisions will help accelerate the transition.

As you head out on this journey, remember how much you love this profession, and more importantly, have fun while you're out there saving the world!

~ Deborah

About the Author

Deborah Dull fell in love with supply chain almost two decades ago over menu planning and workback schedules. She has explored different industries through a supply chain lens at Microsoft, the Bill & Melinda Gates Foundation, and General Electric. She has inspired thousands of supply chain professionals to learn about Circular Supply Chains through keynote speeches, podcasts, and peer-reviewed journals.